Poet
Mo

Cheshire Vol II
Edited by Chris Hallam

 Young**Writers**

First published in Great Britain in 2004 by:
Young Writers
Remus House
Coltsfoot Drive
Peterborough
PE2 9JX
Telephone: 01733 890066
Website: www.youngwriters.co.uk

SB ISBN 1 84460 354 7

Foreword

This year, the Young Writers' 'Poetry In Motion' competition proudly presents a showcase of the best poetic talent selected from over 40,000 up-and-coming writers nationwide.

Young Writers was established in 1991 to promote the reading and writing of poetry within schools and to the youth of today. Our books nurture and inspire confidence in the ability of young writers and provide a snapshot of poems written in schools and at home by budding poets of the future.

The thought effort, imagination and hard work put into each poem impressed us all and the task of selecting poems was a difficult but nevertheless enjoyable experience.

We hope you are as pleased as we are with the final selection and that you and your family continue to be entertained with *Poetry In Motion Cheshire Vol II* for many years to come.

Contents

Alderley Edge School for Girls

Sarah Poe (15)	48
Sarah Aldridge (13)	49
Jessica Lander (12)	49
Alex Barrie (13)	50
Natalie Law (14)	51
Emma King (13)	52
Amy Baston (12)	53
Joanna Lonsdale (12)	54
Emma Wigglesworth (12)	54

All Saints Catholic College

Caroline Hopkins (11)	55
Jodie Brown (11)	55
Amelia Cowburn (12)	56
Adam Noble (13)	56
Lucy Taylor (13)	57
Thomas Bailey (13)	57
Adam Wharmby (13)	58
Shaun O'Neill (13)	58
Scott Wadsworth (11)	59
Christine Cooper (12)	60
Kirsty-Leanne Charlesworth (13)	60

Altrincham Grammar School for Boys

David Williams (12)	61
Alex Stewart (11)	62
Joel McLoughlin (11)	62
Philip Marchant (12)	63
Christian Sadler (11)	63
Joe Hesford (11)	64
Andrew Veitch (12)	65
Matthew Walley (11)	65
James Favas (12)	66
Sam Rogers (12)	67
Carl Vernon (12)	68
Tim Evans (12)	69
Henry Brown (11)	69
Daniel Melling (12)	70
Jonathan Faupel (12)	71

Dominic Bates (11)	72
Alex Cusick (12)	72
Tom Cottrell (11)	73
Philip Conti-Ramsden (11)	73
Alex Barker (11)	74
Michael Booth (11)	75
Michael Shaw (12)	76
Hedayat Javidi (12)	77

Coppenhall High School

Byrone Heywood (12)	77
Carl Plant	78
Laura Rowley (11)	78
Sarajane Passey (11)	79
Jamie Dutton (12)	79
Hayley Maginnis (15)	80
Ben Harrop (12)	80
Claire Pettitt (13)	81
David Bennion (12)	81
Mark Triner (13)	82
Jessica Heath (12)	82
Emily Bennett (12)	83
Kowser Ahmed (12)	83
Thomas Butters (11)	84
Matthew Hallyburton (11)	84
Abigail Burrow (11)	85
Joe Gardiner (11)	85
Ben Grice (12)	86
Samantha Cartwright (11)	86
Sam Cormack (12)	87
Julian Powell (11)	87
Rhys Ingham (11)	88
Stephanie Clayton (11)	88
Leanne Chesters (12)	89
Ashley Scoffin	89
Chris Halford (12)	90
Anthony Jamhour (11)	90
Alexander David King (13)	91
Laura Rowlands (11)	91
Krystal Latham (13)	92
Matthew Bennett (11)	92

Sam Jamhour (14)	93
Chloe Critchlow (11)	93
Frances Ryder (13)	94
Claire Baker (11)	94
Sharna Gallagher (11)	95
Christopher Wilcock (12)	95
Chris Hulme (13)	96
Tom Darby (12)	96
Benjamin Ollier (12)	97
Jamielee Challinor (12)	97
Sammie McGowan (12)	98
Roxanne Mooney (11)	98
Lauren May (11)	99
Sarah King-Evans (11)	99
Natasha Vyse (13)	100
Natalie Williams (11)	101
Emma Triner (11)	102
Emma Giltrap (12)	102
Tiffany McCann (12)	103
Craig Minshull (11)	103
Katie Bates (12)	104
Samantha Goodwin (11)	104
Jade O'Reilly (13)	105
Zach Chambers (11)	105
Christopher Dunn (13)	106
Michael Ellis (11)	106
Billy Clews (14)	107
Stephen Pietrusiak (11)	107
Sally-Ann Pleavin (13)	108
Jemma Rowley (11)	108
James Webb (13)	109
Stephanie Jones (11)	109
Rhianwen Haynes (13)	110
Stefan Phillips (12)	111
Michaela Entwistle (12)	111
Dan Sherratt (13)	112
Steven Parker (12)	112
Jodie Grocott (12)	113
Melanie Challinor (12)	113
Becky Cort (12)	114
Aimee Woolley (13)	114
Emma Kennedy (12)	115

Hyde Technology School

Ryles Park High School

David Mellor (12)	185
Sarah Buckley (13)	186
Jake Cotterill (12)	186
Casey Harrison (12)	187
Amy Curley (12)	187
Tasha Clowes (12)	187
Wayne Woodward (14)	188
Erin Brooks (14)	189
Daniel Burns (12)	189
Christopher Douglas (12)	189
Christopher Huxley (13)	190
Hannah Lee (13)	190
Rebecca Whitehurst (14)	190
Gavin Murphy (13)	191
Harry Taylor (13)	191
Kayliegh Rowe & Stacey Brown (13)	192
Christine Postlewhite (12)	192
Stuart Reid (13)	193
Nicole Weaver (13)	193
Charlotte Crooks (12)	194
Dale Sullivan (14)	194
Simon Walker (13)	195
Kimberley Huxley (12)	195

St Ambrose College, Altrincham

George Massey (11)	196
Robert Edwards (11)	197
Ben Magill (12)	197
Sean Wright (11)	198
Nicholas Henry (11)	198
Aaron Ward (12)	199
Martin Solomon (11)	200
Joseph Cooper (11)	200
Daniel Gunn (11)	201
Alex Waterhouse (11)	201
Tom Gurrie (11)	202
Aaron Gibbons (12)	202
Christian Hickson (11)	203
Mark Arnfield (11)	203
James Carr (11)	204
Alex Hartley (11)	204

Matthew Baker (11)	205
James Taberham (12)	205
Marek Walker (11)	206
Thomas Appleton (11)	206
Dan Cere (12)	207
Ryan Moffatt (12)	207

Tarporley Community High School

Vicky Armstrong (13)	208
George White (12)	208
Lois Walley (12)	209
Daniel Hopwood (12)	209
Jess Brownlee (13)	210
Alexander Gittins (12)	210
Richard Pover (12)	211
Georgina Dotchin (12)	212
David Barden (12)	212
David Clarke (12)	213
Ryder Caldwell (12)	213
Rachel O'Neill (12)	214
Holly Davies (12)	214
Jessica Craven (12)	215
Eleanor Cheeseman (12)	215
Rachel Glover (12)	216
Myles Carr (12)	216
Toni Burton (12)	217
Jacob Hall (12)	217
Stephen Jennings (12)	218
Jonty Deynem (12)	218
Stacey Munro (12)	219
Bethany Andrew (12)	219
Laura Rourke (13)	220
Eric Jones (12)	220
Kelly Wynne (15)	221
Sarah Mills (13)	221
Zara Welch (12)	222
Charlotte Lister (12)	223
Cherry Swift (12)	224
Hannah Aftab (12)	224
David Worrall (12)	225
Nathan Seeney (12)	226

The Poems

The Exam

Off you go, you may start,
I can feel the racing of my heart.
It's bouncing like a jelly bean,
The fastest one I've ever seen.

The paper seems so very thick,
I suddenly feel so very sick.
I want someone to take me home,
But it feels like I'm all alone.

Smartest kids nearly done,
But not me, I've just begun.
I should have done more revision,
Like English stories and maths division.

Stop! The test is now complete,
I'll take your sheets, I hope it's neat.
Next time I'll revise,
No matter the book size.

Emma Lally (11)
Abbey Gate College

A Canal

The canal flows and flows,
Collecting rain water on its way.
Leaves floating on the surface,
Gliding further each day.

The rain falls into the canal,
Making ripples in the water,
While animals look for a place
To shelter from the rain.

The world around might change
And animals may come and go,
But the canal stays the same,
Flowing one way
And another.

Laura McKenzie (11)
Abbey Gate College

The Eagle

He looks down on us,
like a king on a throne.
His feathers are a glowing cloak,
made of golden thread.
His talons cannot wait until . . .
they dig into an animal's skin.
Waiting up there in his blue kingdom,
his eyes search the world beneath him.

He soars back to his nest,
in the tallest tree of the forest.
There his hungry chicks await him,
they shriek with beaks agape,
longing for their first meal.
Contented, they feed on the corpse,
but soon he will go,
to prey on some other foe.

James Roden (11)
Abbey Gate College

The Hockey Match

It's my first match and I'm raring to play,
I've been in suspense all day,
The whistle goes and we're off,
Like pigs to a trough!

The sound of crashing sticks,
As the teams mix,
The ball gets hit again and again into the goal,
Soon there will be a hole!
If you get hurt in the game,
Don't make a fuss, there's no one to blame.

Charlotte Davies (12)
Abbey Gate College

Which Side Are You On?

Have you ever noticed,
In our right-handed world,
If you dare use your left,
Then the insults are hurled?

Have you ever noticed,
Lefties are not 'correct'?
Foods that are leftover
Are ones we don't select.

Have you ever noticed,
If you have two left feet,
What it really means is
Ya can't dance to the beat!

Have you ever noticed,
Unless it's misconstrued,
The French say left is 'gauche',
It means you're rather rude.

Have you ever noticed,
Left field's nowhere near?
Left-handed compliments
Are never quite sincere.

Have you ever noticed,
Left's unfortunate plight?
It's discrimination,
'Cause it just isn't *right!*

Allana Stevenson (11)
Abbey Gate College

The Hallowe'en Nightmare

The Hallowe'en nightmare is coming,
The headless horseman is near.
A black cat is walking past,
A big sign of terror.
Bats are squawking past our door,
A real sign of terror.
Pumpkins shining in a window,
Their grin is a sign of terror.
The Devil welcomes you to the dreaded land,
A massive sign of terror.
The doorknob pounds,
A big rush of fear,
Like it or not, the trick or treaters are here!

Matthew Daulby (11)
Abbey Gate College

Rivers

Rivers are cool
Rivers are blue
Rivers have feelings just like you
Rivers are soft
Rivers are calm
Rivers are cold when they touch your arm

Rives are young
Rivers are old
Some are mighty, some are bold

Some are clean
Some are dirty
Some lead a life dark and murky.

Alastair Buckle (11)
Abbey Gate College

The Catherine Wheel

It ignites up the blue paper,
Lifts its body up into the sky,
It pops, burps, twists and turns,
Winding itself round as the paper it burns.

Rainbow of colours hit the blue sky,
Zigzags of purple around us they fly.
Starbursts of light, arches of gold,
They sound loud and harsh and echo bold.

Screams and cries
Ahs and oohs,
Started the moment the match hit the fuse.

Round like a circle,
Shaped like a snail,
The wheel starts to stutter
And becomes very frail.

The fizz starts to whisper,
The circle starts to fade,
Blank now, no colours, dull now, no spark,
All of the light is drenched in the dark.

Eleanor Gibson (11)
Abbey Gate College

The Life Of A Football

I spend most of my time on the pitch,
It's not very nice getting hit.
I wish I had got picked to be on the pitch,
When England won 5-1 against Germany.
I've been kicked by all the top kits,
Like Arsenal, Liverpool and United,
But my biggest wish is to be a kid
And play for Man United.

Jonathan Clarke (11)
Abbey Gate College

Living Inside A Grandfather Clock

Living inside a grandfather clock,
Tick-tock, tick-tock.
It wakes me up, every time it's o'clock,
Tick-tock, tick-tock.
It's so hard to sleep, the clock keeps going,
Tick-tock, tick-tock.
The noise is annoying, my anger is showing,
Tick-tock, tick-tock.
It's really *hard* to concentrate,
Tick-tock, tick-tock.
This grandfather clock is messing with fate,
Tick-tock! Tick-tock!

Crash! Thud! Wallop! Clang!
Clash! Boom! Poof! Bang!

A word of advice, (if you can read!),
I'm telling you now, please take heed,
Never go and try to lock . . .
Yourself inside a *grandfather clock!*

Harry Bandell (11)
Abbey Gate College

The Life Of A Football

The ball bounces up and down like a clown,
Its penetrating action is amazing,
As it pelts towards the goal,
Like a cannonball shooting through the air,
It will go until it hits its destination,
The goal.

Tom Ogden (11)
Abbey Gate College

Tell Me There Is A Place

Tell me there's a place where all people go,
Where political lies and social problems
Don't trouble their lives,
Where crimes don't sweep onto the streets,
Taking people's lives.
Where men don't make other men black and blue,
Where war does not happen.

On every night when a baby dies,
A mummy cries.
Grandpa says they are happy now,
They sit with God in paradise,
They have angels' wings.

But somehow it makes me feel like ice,
Why did they have to die?
Is there a place where people and animals don't die?

Tell me there is a place.

Oliver Makower (11)
Abbey Gate College

The Catherine Wheel

Catherine wheel spinning round and round,
Sparks flying; red, orange and yellow.
Radiating circles, bigger and bigger,
Golden tail blazing in the night.
Revolving, rotating, glistening light.
She twirls around, a beautiful dance,
Shining brightly in a trance.
Until she fades away into the darkness.

Arthur Thomas (11)
Abbey Gate College

At Christmas

I'm so excited, 'The time has come,
For you to put your stocking out,' says Mum.
On the fireplace the sherry, mince pie and carrots lie,
If I hide behind the sofa I might see his face.

Up to bed I have to go,
Hoping that I'll wake up to lots of snow.
I wonder if Father Christmas will like the lights,
When he is looking down from great heights.

Tomorrow when I wake, I can't wait to see
What he has left for me,
By the tree,
Christmas dinner is always great,
Turkey, sprouts, carrots on my plate.

Jessica Richards (11)
Abbey Gate College

The Haunted House

Seeking blood, moans and a scream,
calls for help are not what they seem.
Darkness noises come from inside
and if you go in, you're in for a ride.
Deep howls scare, walk in with a care,
the ghosts are near and the risk is sheer.
This house on a hill, it's there to kill,
if you go in, there's no chance you can win
against this house, you're as weak as a mouse.
A mouse is small, a mouse can hide,
but it can't escape, the haunted ride!

Joshua Nock (11)
Abbey Gate College

The Fight!

The cat, the dog and the mouse,
Start a tremendous fight.
It all starts off,
In the middle of the night.

The cat (in silence),
Creeps after the mouse,
When all of a sudden,
Flies into the room,
A dog, tall but strong,
Whiskers a-quiver,
A situation of
Dreadful doom.

The dog barks, the cat shrieks,
The mouse shrinks swiftly away.
The cat follows racing and hissing,
But the dog gets bored with the fray.

Jennie Mayers-Worrall (11)
Abbey Gate College

A Wonderful Ride In The Countryside!

Hills, loaves of bred,
on and on they go.
Rivers like long snakes,
slithering as they flow.

In the streams are silver minnows,
underneath the weeping willows here and there.
The smell of natural forests,
is the smell of fresh air.

Snowflake keeps pounding on and on,
she doesn't stop, she just keeps going,
Like a white velvet curtain,
her mane is flowing.

Emily Burnett (11)
Abbey Gate College

The Rugby World Cup

It's October 2003 we are ready and up,
Australia the destination for rugby world cup,
Every rugby nation
Is in total celebration!
Fans from all around
Are down under Aussie bound.
Georgia, Japan and Scotland,
France, Ireland and England.
42 days of ruck and maul,
42 days of giving all.
Tackle, drive, score a try,
Sweat, pain, more than a few will cry.
Wallabies, All Blacks and Springbock,
Nail-biting 80 minutes watching the clock.
Wilkinson, Johnstone, Back and Kay,
Hoping the rose will bloom on the final day.
Scots, Irish and Welsh will run and run,
Hoping for glory in the sun.
The winners will not be boys but men,
The world will be in union once again.
The Webb Ellis trophy will only be lifted by the best,
The team who win the cup have passed the test
And when the dust has settled, it will be the same,
The pride is in playing, playing the game
And when I go on the rugby field at Abbey Gate,
I think I might play in the cup one day, it would be my fate!

Scott Jones (12)
Abbey Gate College

The Fairground

The sky was getting darker,
As the night was drawing in.
The moon was shining brightly,
The fun was soon to begin.

We raced along the pavement,
Our coats and scarves all flying,
As we tumbled into the fairground,
Children laughing, shouting and crying.

The rides were so exciting,
The stalls so funny and thrilling,
We spent out money so quickly,
Children running, excited and willing.

Time to go home, tired and hungry,
Heavy, laden, legs all aching,
Home at last to warm, snug beds,
Morning will soon come, a new day waking.

Conor Greenwood (11)
Abbey Gate College

The Seas

The sea is calm lapping against the bay,
It could lead no creature, alive astray
As night falls a storm breaks,
Creating havoc beneath the wakes,
Thunder rings through the air,
Lightning crashes with no lives to spare,
We're as far out to sea, a fisherman's boat is rocking then
All of a sudden the storm dies down
And people stop to think twice about fleeing the town.

Thomas Donaldson (11)
Abbey Gate College

The Why Baby

Why are you waking me when I was asleep?
I was dreaming of Little Bo Peep and her sheep.

Why are you feeding me this horrid food?
It's enough to put me in a mood.

Why are you stopping me from crawling on the floor?
When all I want to do is get through the door.

Why are you putting me in this clean tidy dress?
It's taken me so much effort to make such a mess.

Why are you sitting me next to my dad?
He's watching the football and if I cry he'll get mad.

Why are you putting me to bed when I'm wide awake?
Asleep this morning you woke me for goodness sake.

Why are doing all this to me?
Why don't you just leave me be!

Kate Mort (11)
Abbey Gate College

Parrot

Oh colourful, colourful bird
How do you hear my every word?
What should I say and what should I play?
Should I play hangman? I'm stuck what to say,

Can I play with you?
Can I hold you?
But no, it's time for me to go,
Oh, how I will miss you so.

Helen Palmer (11)
Abbey Gate College

Tigers

The tiger, the lord of cats
Better than pussy cats
The lion, the cheetah, many more
Claws of silver maul the floor
Teeth of iron that nothing will withstand
No human nor no iron band

Its coat of fire
Eyes of sapphire
Its tail a perfect orange flame
Flickers with the wind searching to maim
Its roar like thunder
Will split asunder

The tiger, the lord of the cats
Should not feed on lowly rats
He stalks the plains
Setting his aim
On the creature
Unfortunate enough to stray into sight

There is no fight
Nor any competition
Only a repetition
Of what happens every time
For in this rhyme
The tiger is the lord of cats!

Edward Speakman (11)
Abbey Gate College

The Pied Piper

Hamelin Town was full of rats,
The piper came and that was that.
I survived, I am the best!
All the others have gone to rest.

I found a spot, I thought was safe,
I called it, my secret hiding place.
I made a tunnel to a different town,
I left no trace where I went down.

Left alone with only some bait,
I found a way to make an escape.
I climbed a really long steep hill,
All to find my good friend, Will.

We went to a place called Berlin
And met an old wizard called Merlin.
He helped us find our secret powers,
But it took us ages, hours and hours.

James Handley (11)
Abbey Gate College

Waterfalls

Waterfalls are blue,
With diamonds and hue,
With rattling waves
And a sunlit blaze.

Rumbling, tumbling down,
It comes splashing, crashing,
Against the rocks, you hear
A sound of whipping water.

All is calm and safe,
Until you see a water snake!

Julian Buckle (11)
Abbey Gate College

My New School

I'm outside the gates staring up
At my new school.
I go in and go down the drive,
A feel all squeamish as if I'm only five.

A third year leads me up the stairs,
I'm lost, I'm lost, I don't know where to go.
Yes! I've found my form room at last,
Compared to some, I got there quite fast!

Off to English in room four,
The maths, RE and geography,
Lunch is next, chicken nuggets and chips,
The doughnut for pudding has me licking my lips.

Science is next, all afternoon,
In the lab with Bunsen burners and all.
The day has ended, I collect my bag,
When I get out of the gates, I begin to lag.

I stand there, then flump down on the grass,
My mum comes and I get in the car.
I'm glad my first day has gone, but oh no!
I've got another nine months to go!

William Hockedy (11)
Abbey Gate College

The White Horses

White horses, crashing through the blue,
Roaring over the misty sea,
Great rows upon rows of beauty,
Glory and power, taking over the mystified oceans.
Approaching the golden kingdom furiously,
Before breaking, falling, dying and ending.

Reached the shore.

Roaring no more.

Tom Giles (11)
Abbey Gate College

Wrexham FC

Why do I support Wrexham FC?
Known as the Dragons,
The team that plays in red and white.
The players that shine at the racecourse are many,
The captain, Ferguson, big Dennis the defender,
So solid at the back,
Andy Morrell, our top scorer,
Who has now been sold.
Andy Dibble, who has hands
Like tennis racquets,
What a goalie he is.
This is why I support Wrexham FC,
The best team in the land,
The Dragons,
Come on you reds!

Michael Lewis (11)
Abbey Gate College

On A Boat

The waves are giant,
like white horses at a gallop.
On my boat I am dwarfed
by their magnificent splendour.

The storm dies down,
relief, as the waves diminish.
Suddenly, I notice a leak,
cold water splashes around my feet.

The boat starts to sink,
the freezing water grips my legs.
I'm going under, down with my boat,
to rest on the sea floor for evermore.

Jeremy Waterworth (11)
Abbey Gate College

Parents Kissing

It started by Dad
Dragging Mum across
The hall, no one
Could get past,
I was really appalled.

Frankly I think it's wrong,
For people with four children
To go on kissing so long!
'Mum, Janice is chasing me!' I shout.

'Dad, I need you,
I need you,
I need you *now!*
Rachel is being stupid!
Put Mum down, please and help me!

Mum, you've made him red-faced,
Dad, you've made her all giggly.
No one should do this,
It makes us all wiggly.'

Frances Manton (11)
Abbey Gate College

Water

Hardly moving, lying still,
Gently lapping at the sides.
Glittering, shimmering still until,
I start moving with the tides.

Rippling, waving effortlessly,
Clear as the blue sky above.
Reflecting surroundings perfectly
And the natural images of love.

Emma Williams (11)
Abbey Gate College

The Glaramara Challenge

We went on a trip to Glaramara,
I went with my friends and also my father.

We left school, around about three,
Jem, Will, Daulby and me.

We went canoeing on Derwent Water,
We then played football and the dads were slaughtered!

We had to solve problems by making a square,
We were blindfolded, so didn't know who was where.

We went gorge scrambling, it was very wet,
The water was so cold that some got upset.

There were six teams, on this weekend of fun,
We were the happiest cos the challenge we won!

Our team was good, no, our team was great,
If you don't believe us, you can ask Mr H!

James Ivill (11)
Abbey Gate College

Forest Fire

Something's hot and coming
It's silent, too silent
Look out, forest fire
Quick, run like the wind, the fire's coming
Jump like an eagle, the forest fire's coming
Quickly run, run, run!
Keep running, it's coming
Quickly, it's catching
It's almost here, don't look back
It's right behind us!
Stop!
The fire, it's gone . . .

Emily Dyer (11)
Abbey Gate College

I Don't Want This

I was looking out of my cot,
when there was a big person standing over me.
They do this every day,
I wonder why?

It's not like I do something spectacular is it?
I don't do the monkey bars or anything,
then they move me around
and I'm quite happy there.

So I cry and get fed,
that is not what I want.

So they give me a toy,
but I don't like that one,
so I throw it away.

Then they try to put me to sleep in my rocking chair,
but I don't want to go to sleep.
All I want is to be in my cot
and play with all my toys.

So I cry again
and they read me a story,
but I don't want a story.

So I reached out and got the story and threw it away,
then they got my rattle out,
that was my favourite toy.

They put me in my cot
and the first thing I did was go to sleep!

Hannah Dyer (11)
Abbey Gate College

Me

What on earth's that you're throwing over me?
You always do this when I'm on the settee
And now you're going to snuggle me in deep,
In the hope I'm going to fall asleep.

Well, no, I'm not,
I'm far too hot.

Would you stop blowing me a sloppy kiss,
I want to carry on fiddling with this,
Stop it, please stop it, put me down right now,
Otherwise it's going to cause a great big row.

Hey, I'm hungry,
Mum, I'm hungry.

Mummy, where have you disappeared to?
Please, I really need to speak to you.
Come out now, I'm ready for my tea.

Is this all because you dearly love me?

Rachel Preston (11)
Abbey Gate College

World War I

I am cold, the water is coming into my boots,
People killing and dying; guns being let off.
The noise now getting louder, louder,
Until the noise became quieter.
Then, I felt a bad pain in my back,
I touched my back, blood poured out on my finger.
I took a last glimpse up,
Bodies filled the field, I thought of poppies . . .

Joe Imlach (11)
Abbey Gate College

There Once Was An Old Man
Who Lived On A Hill

There once was an old man who lived on a hill,
He hated the warmth and he hated the chill.
He hated all people when they did lie,
Though he never spoke the truth. His name: Fogi.
He never went outdoors, just stayed there in his room,
Pondering his next plot down there in the gloom.
You see he hated all children and adults as well,
So he devised a plan to make them unwell.
He gathered up mushrooms and sun lotion too
And mashed them together to make a stew!
Later that night he fed it to the town,
To their horror next morning their skin had turned brown.
The entire town had devoured that stew,
Barr one, a blacksmith. His name: Matthew.
He charged up the hill, axe in hand,
To get rid of the man who had plagued the land.
With a slice and a slash the deed was done,
He had saved the land, he had saved everyone!
When he came back, you have not seen such mirth,
You could hear the cheering from Iceland to Perth.
So now you have heard the tale of Fogi and friends
And how a young blacksmith made amends.
But, unfortunately, Fogi's potion had spread too quick,
You could be contaminated with just one lick.
It turned out he wasn't such a bad man,
So now people can get a really good tan!
No one could say whether Fogi was round the bend,
But one thing we can say is that this is . . .
The end!

Liam Warriner (12)
Abbey Gate College

The Ghost Of The Flat Cat

The ghost of the flat cat haunts Highville Road,
Some people say to stop the dreaded sound,
There is a special code.
He miaows, he growls,
He even sometimes groans,
With his spirit reliving the moment
When he became the ghost of Highville Road.

Looking back within the past,
Looking back to as far as the cat could remember,
It was at least December,
He was padding along the ground,
Across the road without a sound.

He saw a light in the distance,
Just around the corner,
You must look what you do when you cross the road,
And that is how he became,
The ghost of the flat cat that haunts Highville Road.

Now what did you learn from that?
You must never trust a cat!

Katherine Aspinall (11)
Abbey Gate College

Forests

Forests are groaning creatures
Tired and exhausted because of their old, creaky trees
Plants and grass as far as the eye can see
Forests have feelings too
In the spring they are bright and ready
In the summer, happy and joyful
In autumn they are sad
To see their leaves disappear
And in the winter they are resting
Waiting for the next year.

Laurence Fryer-Taylor (11)
Abbey Gate College

Cricket Wonders

Cricket is the sport to play;
Keep on batting all the day.
The bowler bowls,
The batsman strikes,
Is it a four? We're not quite sure.
Shot of the day, six they say,
The bowler dreams and hopes of nicks,
Next ball, it's in the slips.
The batsman hits the ball into the air,
Brushing the clouds as it passes by,
The ball lands safely in the fielder's hands,
Bowler appeals for out,
Tricky wicket, but it's out.
Funny old game!
We shout about.

Jordan Baker (11)
Abbey Gate College

The Stars

They sparkle like floating diamonds,
High above my bed,
Giving me comfort,
While I rest my head.

They light the darkness,
Showing me the way,
Helping me to rest myself,
For another day.

I stare up and wonder,
How, far away,
Those stars sit waiting,
For light the next day.

Jade Grimwood (11)
Abbey Gate College

A Day In The Sun

When you wake up on a summer's dawn,
You stretch your arms and yawn
Breathing in the warm, fresh air,
You dress, then saunter down the stair.

You run outside into the sun's rays,
Ready to get burnt by its blaze,
Choosing your spot carefully, you've got a plan,
To bake in the sun so you get a tan.

Alas, you've forgotten something
And now you're peeling,
It's the suncream you've forgotten,
Oh bother, oh rotten.

Now you feel really bad,
To think of that good day you could've had,
Lying in the sun all day
And not worrying about its ray.

The sun is setting in the sky,
You feel like you want to cry,
Very sad, you go to bed,
But dream about the sun instead.

Emily Parkinson (12)
Abbey Gate College

The River

The river flowing fast along the riverbank,
Hitting a couple of rocks, suddenly they sank,
Down the waterfall,
Taking branches big and small.

The river weaved its way to the coast,
Joining other streams to make the most,
Down to the estuary there it came,
The River Thames was its name.

Sam Millington (11)
Abbey Gate College

My Teddy

My teddy, he sits on the window sill
All alone in thought he seems
He looks out on the field
Where our garden lies
And dreams, dreams, dreams

I can only wonder, I can only surmise
What thoughts go on in his head
His eyes black as coal
His fur golden brown
Oh my dear, dear ted

My teddy, he sits on the window sill
As he eyes the clean-cut lawn
He's got a smiley mouth
And a shiny black nose
And he sits there from dusk to dawn
My teddy is more than a toy
On him I can always depend
He sits there still
So patiently
My best, best friend.

Annabelle Edge (11)
Abbey Gate College

The Hunt

Horses running,
Fox's heart racing.
The hounds hear the horn
And start chasing.

Thundering hooves getting louder,
Hounds barking, getting near.
Huntsmen galloping fast,
Will the fox escape from fear?

Sam Williams (11)
Abbey Gate College

Looking Over The World!

I am the sun, who created the world,
I am the sun, who gives light to the world,
But does the world thank me?
No.
Does it look after the world itself?
No.
Men and women destroy the Earth.
As I slowly go down I see,
Mankind hurting animals,
Polluting the world,
Drug dealing and smoking.
Soon there will be no world left
And it will be man's fault.
My rays of light are fading away,
As I am seeing the world being destroyed.
But, my tears are growing and growing,
I will have nothing to look over soon.
All I can do is watch in pain
And hope man will change his ways,
While I am looking over the world.

Hayley Oakes (12)
Abbey Gate College

The Sun Going Into Complete Darkness

Feel the roaring fire
Grow hotter and hotter.

Watch how the flickering flames
Grow higher and higher.

See the sun change the sky
Pink, red then purple.

Hear the howling of the wolves
As they come to play.

Then all you can see is the man on the moon
Sitting in silence and looking down on us, smiling.

Charlotte Kaufman (11)
Abbey Gate College

Pain

The blood, the agony,
The cold sweat dripping down
Your face onto the splintered
Wood panelled floor.
You try to stand but there is no hope,
You remain sitting in the corner
Of the damp, dusty, dim room,
With bloody tatters hanging
Off your trouser leg,
It's getting later,
You're getting weaker,
You don't know how you're going to survive,
You look out of the window listening to the twigs
Of trees clattering and scratching against them,
Then you go blank,
You fall to the floor,
Have you fainted?
Have you died?
What has happened to you?

Charles Rand (12)
Abbey Gate College

Eagle

Soaring through the bright morning sky,
spreading his wings, ready to fly.
Gracefully gliding like a skater on ice,
he swoops around searching for voles and mice.

Suddenly the eagle spots its prey,
he shoots down in a quick display.
Then he dives below in a direct channel,
the bird wings away and captures the small mammal.

And so, the eagle drifts on,
not knowing where it's going to or coming from.
The bird of prey ascends up and away,
living on to hunt another day.

Edward Reid (11)
Abbey Gate College

On Our School Trip

On our school trip to Scarborough
We went into the wood
We lost naughty Will and Tom
But Bart was being good!

Srinath lost his cap
And found it up a tree
So Marcus tried to get it down
That busy little bee!

Srinath started shouting
At Bart for being good
Will and Tom came back
Much later than they should.

Bart Ryan-Beswick (11)
Abbey Gate College

Bonfire Night

Rockets shooting up, high into the night,
Firing out bright coloured puffs of light.

Huge bonfires ablaze, all crackles and heat,
Guy sits on top, flames licking his feet.

Children wrapped up all warm and tight,
All aware of the dangers in sight.

Explosions are blinding; blue, green and red,
Millions of stars falling down on my head.

Alex Sarwar (12)
Abbey Gate College

The Memory

The fields, the grass,
Just a memory.
The sights, the smells,
Just a memory.
The fun, the games,
Just a memory.
The fun in the snow, the campfire's glow,
Just a memory.

I sit in my chair,
My wrinkled hand on a photograph book.
Those young childhood days,
They're just a memory.

Robert Taylor (11)
Abbey Gate College

At The Match

The crowd was roaring,
The fans on their feet,
The songs in the background,
As the teams run onto the pitch.

The chants around the stadium,
The players warming up,
The ref blows his whistle
And the battle is about to start.

Joseff Lyddon (12)
Abbey Gate College

Before School!

Wakey, wakey,
Autumn school day again,
Quick, get up and dressed,
Ready for out in the rain.

'Your shirt is clean,
Your tie is there!
Wear your skirt -
Don't go bare!'

Breakfast's ready,
Toast is on the table,
Jam, honey or butter,
As fast as you're able!

Finally!
Bag in jumble,
Hair all a state,
Jump on at the stop,
Because the bus won't wait!

Alice Witter (12)
Abbey Gate College

Christmas Is Near!

The wonderful time of Christmas is near,
With decorations and good cheer.
The nights are colder, frosty and clean,
A crisp white Christmas would be a dream.
Let's wrap our presents under the tree,
Children are happy and full of glee,
For Santa is busy with Christmas toys,
It's so exciting for all girls and boys.
We'll put up stockings by the burning fire,
The anticipation of joy couldn't be higher.
I love the special feast on my favourite day,
Would I swap it all for summer?
No way!

Sam Houston (12)
Abbey Gate College

My Autumn Garden

Autumn is here,
The leaves slowly swirl round,
Onto the wet, dewy grass,
Going through the foggy mist,
Long shadows cover the ground,
The smell of log fires all around,
Brown leaves cover the floor,
Robins fly about
And squirrels scurry for food,
Days get shorter,
The sun gets lower,
Spiders' webs glisten,
With the grass swaying in the wind,
Toadstools come overnight,
Mushrooms appear in the lawn,
Heather comes into the pots
And winter is on its way.

Abigail Hardman (12)
Abbey Gate College

Alone

Sitting there all by herself
Listening to all the gunshots in the background
She just sits there and doesn't shout for help

Everyone panicking and running from place to place
Screaming and trying to find their families
Whilst she just sits there not moving an inch

In the end she moves from their sides
Finally realising they will not come back
She grabs her bear and starts to walk away

She turns back one last time and sees their faces staring into space
Her brother, her sister, her mum and her dad
She then realises how alone she is.

Liz Walker (13)
Abbey Gate College

Lunchtime

Standing in the playground,
Looking at the trees.
Children all around me,
Playing in the breeze.

Tugging at my trousers,
'Will you help me please?
Johnny's fallen over
And got blood all on his knees.'

Throwing stones for hopscotch,
Chasing the football.
Skipping ropes and marbles,
Handstands against the wall.

Whistle finally blows time
And we race up to the door.
Coats and hats are hung up,
But most lie on the floor!

Lunchtime is now over
And lessons have begun.
Time for me to rest my feet,
My lunchtime job is done.

Amy Middlehurst (12)
Abbey Gate College

Three Spirits

We travel together, my brother, sister and me,
I'm Death, my brother is Fate, my sister Destiny.
You try to avoid us, but we don't know why,
You say we live in caves, on mountains, or in the sky.

We don't! We follow you and everybody, waiting to meet you,
If you try running away at night, don't, we never sleep.
My brother and me we'll give you a gift,
Something we hope you will like.

When the time is right and we all agree,
You will hear a knock at the door, and that is me
And when that happens you have no hope.
One word of advice, hide, don't make a sound,
But we three can be nice and kind,
Or have only one thing in mind . . .

We travel together, my sister, brother and me,
My brother, sister and me, we could be your destiny.

Thomas Broomhall (12)
Abbey Gate College

The Lunch Menu

On Monday we have pasta and doughnuts,
A girl found an earwig in hers once.

On Tuesday we have lasagne and trifle,
They look as if they have been put in the liquidiser.

On Wednesday we have chicken nuggets and chips,
They look as if they have been there for weeks.

On Thursday we have cowboy pie and chocolate cake,
They look like a big pile of brown gooey mud.

Friday is the worst day of all, it is called the Friday surprise,
In this they put all the leftover food from the past few weeks.

Laura Knowles (13)
Abbey Gate College

My Black Friend

Black as midnight is he,
Fast as a dart, skimming through the air,
Eyes like glinting stars, chocolate-brown
And glossy as conkers on an autumn day.

His nose is also shiny and wet to touch,
His tail is bushy as a fox's brush.

He dashes round the field, barking,
Chasing wild animals.
He retrieves lost tennis balls in long grass and hedges.
He leaves cute footprints on the kitchen floor,
After rolling around in mud
And no one who saw them would guess the size of him!

His ears flop around his beautifully-shaped head . . .
Until he hears the slightest sound
And they prick up, alert,
There is nothing nicer than to stroke his velvet ears.

He is a four-footed member of the family, loved by all,
His name is Jazz -

The best dog in the world!

Tom Bate (12)
Abbey Gate College

A Poem About A Poem

Do poems have a point?
Yes, maybe, or no.
Some think they might,
But others don't know.

What do these things do?
Disturb, move or cheer?
I don't have a clue,
I find them unclear.

Should poetry be sung
To music, perhaps?
And does it belong
In anthems or raps?

Understanding is rare
And the rhymes disappoint,
So the question's still there:
Do poems have a point?

Eva Binks (13)
Abbey Gate College

Silence Of War

The darkened wall stood towering high,
Clearly cracked with age,
Catching the eye and landscape around it.
The army that stood behind,
Built up with fear,
Swords at the ready,
No one moved,
Silence enclosed everything.
Suddenly, out of the blue,
A single arrow flew over
And pierced the heart of an innocent man,
First of many wasted lives.

Jack Dawson (13)
Abbey Gate College

The Cycle Of Seasons

In the sunshine everything is calm,
Over the hills the birds peacefully fly.
The flowers spread their petals proudly
And snakes lie sunbathing on rocks.

Then, when the leaves fall,
Nature replaces its greens with colours of gold.
Nuts and fruit fall from the trees
And as rain falls, squirrels prepare for winter.

The land changes colour again,
A white layer so beautiful to the eyes,
Covers the dying gold of the earth,
But the pure blanket hides the icy danger.

Just as the earth seems to die away,
The brightly coloured flowers return.
The sun happily melts the snow
And grass returns to that welcoming green.

Even though the birds now feed their young,
They know the unwanted coldness will return.
Every year they feel like this
And we call it the cycle of seasons.

Leonie Geenen (13)
Abbey Gate College

The Water House

Across the fields and down the stream,
Up the hill and along the path,
In summer, winter, spring and autumn,
It stands there all alone,
On the verge of falling apart.

The walls inside are damp and dingy,
The banisters are rotten and worn,
As a family of mice make their nest,
Upon a piece of tattered carpet,
Like otters they scrimmage for bedding.

The windows are smashed
And glass is scattered across the tile floor like shrapnel,
The kitchen carries a distinctive smell
Of raw fish from which came the sudden shock,
That something is there.

The house carries a presence,
As if somebody still lives there,
You have to pass their law,
As they were in charge.

Outside, the chimney has collapsed
And the door is rough and battered,
The garden is overgrown like a jungle,
As at night you can hear the screeches of the crickets,
Like the roar of lions.

The stream running by,
Lead out to the village,
But nobody ever ventured up the river,
To the water house.

Joshua Hardman (13)
Abbey Gate College

Street Football

I think football is great
And I like to play out till late.
I want to play all night,
But come in when there's no light.

We use jumpers as the goals,
Even though they're full of holes.
We kick-off from the middle
And then I start to dribble.

I go to make a pass,
But have to avoid the glass.
Jimmy Smith crosses the ball,
We watch as it hits the wall.

It bounces once, it bounces twice,
I go to kick, but only slice.
It hits a pothole
And yes, I've scored a goal!

From the goal kick the ball goes far,
It gets burst, by a passing car,
We wander home and the final score,
Turned out to be a one-all draw.

Curtis Harman (13)
Abbey Gate College

The Spider

It sits in the corner
And doesn't move;
It watches children play.
Its cobweb is home to many flies,
That have all been wrapped in silk.

Its eight hairy legs
And its big fat body
Can send a chill down any spine.
It crawls away to find a different place,
To build another web.

When you think that it has finally gone,
It will always come back again,
To haunt you;
And sit in the same old place,
Watching time go by.

Jenny Skues (13)
Abbey Gate College

Skiing

Tall, green grass laden with powdery snow blurred past me,
Looking ahead it seemed there was an iced-over rocky precipice,
But it was a steeper passage swept clean of snow,
No crisp, sweet snow here, just ice.

The sun shone brightly and reflected off the snow, dazzling your eyes,
Touching a branch of a tree, sent an avalanche of snow
down my back,
All I could hear was the sound of my skis gliding along,
Never slowing, never stopping.

Where was I now? I had no idea,
But what reason was there for me to worry?
I was lost in a magical world,
The magical world of snow.

Rob Smith (13)
Abbey Gate College

The Match

A rumble of legs stampeded towards me,
They galloped on and then came a call.
The mass of people turned and ran on,
Chasing a small black and white ball.

The ball was kicked high into the air,
Like an eagle it soared through the sky.
Suddenly it turned and glided down,
And landed at the feet of a different guy.

Cheers came from all around,
As a man in red and of six foot two,
Pushed past me and carried on.
There was nothing I could do.

The whistle blew,
Then came a groan,
A man was sent off,
All the people gave a moan.

A man stepped up,
The ball was put in its place.
It was hit, like a leopard
It leapt up into space.

It plundered into the netting,
Then came a shout,
The reds had won,
There was no doubt.

I was a red.

Philip Kingsley (13)
Abbey Gate College

The Canal

I live right next to a canal,
As I look out of my window I see it every day,
It travels along far, far away,
Everybody loves the canal, they all shout and say,
It reminds you of the sea and walking along the bay.

The canal is very calm, peaceful and quiet,
It has colours of a chocolate bar, brown and white.
The surroundings make the canal centre of attention,
The people come and walk to see an attraction.

Many friends will sing and will want to play,
Seagulls, fish, ducks and swans will all come this way.
Especially when the rain makes ripples when it comes down,
It's a sign that the canal is nearly beginning to drown!

The canal always looks lovely whether rain or shine,
Whether the water's rough or calm, it's always fine.
The canal gives someone or something pleasure and delight,
This happens day by day from morning till night.
That's why I live right next to a canal.

Kirsty McKenzie (13)
Abbey Gate College

Inspiring Death

I wandered lonely under the midnight sky,
As cars and animals drove and scurried by.
My heart was beating as slow as a tortoise's walk,
All I wanted to do was sit and talk.
My pace became slower as I watched the moon shine
And I wished that someday its glow would be mine.
The stars sparkled wonderfully bright,
They brought a smile to my face and filled me with delight.
My clothes were dripping wet as I strolled through the rain
And through my heart shot an immediate pain.
I felt so lonely and full of fear,
If only my lover had not been so dear.
Friends had been so trustworthy, then so evil,
Now they have made me feel so feeble.
I looked around and saw many people who were so meek,
That's when I knew I was terribly weak.
I felt foolish like a small child,
My mind was so mixed up that I went wild.
Suddenly I had an awful urge
And from under a lorry did I submerge.

Stephanie Coulter (13)
Abbey Gate College

Waiting For Power

We were all happy
sitting around the TV,
in a warm room,
full of light.

Then it happened,
the lights went out,
horror struck us,
it was a *power cut*.

All you could hear
was the wind howling like a wolf.
You could hear people
talking in alarm;
then, the opening of doors,
the clanging of chairs.

We checked the fuse box,
it was not that,
our fears had been confirmed.

We all waited anxiously,
whilst Mum calls the power company.

They say it will be hours,
so we get out the candles and wait for power,
waiting for the darkness to return to light,
waiting for the cold to return to warmth.

Oliver Bates (13)
Abbey Gate College

Far, Far Away

It was a cold December night
When I decided to go away
Far, far away
I wrote a letter to the neighbour
Saying not to bother calling me
As I would be going away
Far, far away
I stepped out into the night air
And walked away from the house
Where I had spent the last ten years
I was going far, far away
I walked the dark, snow-covered streets
Wondering where to go
When I saw a black taxi by the road
I stopped the driver
And told him to take me somewhere
'Where d'you mean, mate?' he asked
'Somewhere far, far away,' I said
And so he drove me
From north to south, from west to east
As we passed each village and town, I sighed
Knowing each place was nice
But it wasn't far, far away
Eventually we stopped
In a small field next to a Cliff side
The driver said, 'Is this far enough, mate?'
'Yes,' I replied, before getting out
As I looked around me, I finally knew
That I was, without a doubt . . .
Far, far away.

Adam Thornton (13)
Abbey Gate College

A Sad Injury

As free as the wind
Speeding down the half-pipe ramp
Nine hundred degrees having just been spun
And the crowd cheers for the skateboarding champ
His skill so tremendous that it seems
That the skateboard is a part of his body
His level of talent beyond wildest dreams
Beyond that of everybody

Crash

Lying now in the hospital ward
Nothing to distract the pain
After falling off his skateboard
It's such a shame
Once he was flying high
But because of gravity's law
He's fractured his thigh
And will be skateboarding no more.

Julian Moore (13)
Abbey Gate College

Closing Hole

As I stood at the final hole,
I gazed down at the pennant.
Its pinnacle swished in the breeze;
I clenched the rubber grip and swung back.

I sauntered down the verdant fairway
And peered over the nearest mound,
Then saw my diminutive sphere,
I clenched the rubber grip and swung back.

I strode onto the smooth green;
My feet sank into the leafy ground.
I clenched the rubber grip and swung back;
The ball rolled and sank into the crack.

Lawrence Gibson (13)
Abbey Gate College

Twin Towers

Remember, remember the 11th of September,
When thousands lost their lives.
The chaos and destruction caused by two planes,
Travelling in straight lines.

On board, the passengers and the crew,
Praying to God to be spared.
The hijackers on those planes,
Never even cared.

People of New York stopped and stared
At each beautiful building.
Now smoke and flames consume them,
Sirens and screaming, bodies seen leaping.

The terrorists thought they had escaped,
But they will be haunted by this very day.
They hide in their caves in deserts afar,
But they will be caught, all the people pray.

Families mourn their loved ones lost,
They visit Ground Zero to see where they died.
All they can feel is pain and sorrow,
All they can do is watch and cry.

Spare a thought for innocent gone,
For mothers, fathers, daughters and sons.
Their deaths will be remembered forever and ever,
May God rest their souls . . . every one.

Lara Scholz (13)
Abbey Gate College

Autumn

Darker mornings,
Morning mist almost frosty,
Weak sunshine,
Low autumn sun
And a nip in the air.

Fox prints in the dew,
Spiders' webs shimmering,
Sleepy hedgehogs,
Hibernating animals,
Hoarding squirrels.

Conkers glistening,
Small boys gathering,
Kicking up leaves,
Throwing sticks at trees,
Squabbles in the playground.

Apples ripe and juicy,
Blackberries sweet,
Rustling leaves tumbling down,
Trees becoming bare,
Harvest moon has a yellow glow.

As I sit by the fire,
An owl flies past
And hoots in the night,
Autumn is here.

James Andrews (13)
Abbey Gate College

Why?

Oh no, he's gone!
He's gone, he's gone.
Why me? Why me?
Why has this been done?

The car, it was too fast,
Why did he step out?
I wish I hadn't been there,
But now it's all in the past.

I screamed when I saw the car,
Why didn't he listen?
I did all I could,
However, he went too far.

The ambulance came, but they were too late,
Why didn't they save him?
Why? Why? Why?
Why were they too late?

Samantha Cope (13)
Abbey Gate College

Do You Love Me?

Deep oceans of blue,
They are always so true.
Never do they leak a lie
And never will they let my heart die.
For they are the oceans of you,
That will never again be blue.
Why do oceans lose their colour?
Their love must be fuller.
For I will fill your oceans of blue,
Because my love is true.
Please tell me in those oceans of blue,
Do you love me too?

Sarah Poe (15)
Alderley Edge School for Girls

I Can't Imagine What It's Like . . .

I've tried to find the words
to say what's in my mind
I can't imagine what it's like . . .
to be without mankind

We have all heard of poverty
we have all heard of thirst
but have you ever thought
to put someone else first?

I can only imagine
what it's like to be alone
how it feels to do without
how to get by on my own

So tomorrow, smile at someone
take the time to think of others
there are people starving out there
and people with no mothers.

Sarah Aldridge (13)
Alderley Edge School for Girls

I'm In Love

A romantic boat trip drifting into the night,
Lapping on the dark sea, with just candlelight,
Waiting for your dazzling date to come and sit beside you,
A delicious meal just for two,
A dark red napkin shaped like a heart,
We love each other madly, we will never be apart,
Love songs playing to the beat of the boat,
I shiver a little, he hands me his coat,
I get a bit closer, he surprises me with a pretty flower,
While I'm in love with him, I feel full of power,
I look at him, he looks at me and we lean for each other,
The best kiss, the best feeling, with the best lover!

Jessica Lander (12)
Alderley Edge School for Girls

The Space Shuttle That Never Returned

The amazing seven astronauts,
Shot up into space one day,
Mission controllers lost all contact,
But were they on their way?

As they re-entered Earth's orbit,
They faced their fears and fate,
Death stared at them for a minute,
Would their loved ones remember this date?

2pm, British time,
Debris flooded the Texan sky,
Many saw it happen,
They knew that the seven would die.

America was plunged into mourning,
As it came up on the news,
What had happened was the question
And many were now confused.

Was it human error
Or just a big mistake?
Questions lie unanswered,
Until this very date.

A damaged wing on lift-off
Was thought to be the blame,
Space research has to continue but . . .
Life will never be the same.

Alex Barrie (13)
Alderley Edge School for Girls

The Remembrance

9.04 in the morning
A perfectly normal day
New Yorkers working as usual
Hurrying on their way

Suddenly a shout from the street
Made the fireman stare
His video recorder was scanning
Directly into the glare

There was a plane flying low
Heading straight for the towers
It hit with a bang and everyone turned
An attack against US power

There followed a very long silence
While people realised in fright
That people were dying around them
They started running and pushing in flight

Oh my gosh there was another
That hit the huge tower's twin
What had they done to deserve this?
Sure America wasn't going to let them win

My heart beats faster
I can't believe my eyes
What a disaster
There are people falling from the skies

Thousands of people were killed
Osama bin Laden is to blame
Let's hope that God helps us to forgive him
And that nothing like this happens again.

Natalie Law (14)
Alderley Edge School for Girls

Curiosity Killed My Cat

It only happened yesterday
I still can't face the fact
At that tragic moment my world went black
For this accident I thought at first was an act

It happened just outside my bedroom window
I'll never forget that day
Many tears were shed
Now he is buried in my garden where he will forever lay

It was early in the morning when it happened
The whole world was about to wake
Popcorn only went across the road
This turned out to be his fatal mistake

A person in a car driving too fast
Didn't see my Popcorn, a white, fluffy cat
Smack! He was hit to the ground
Although Popcorn was struck, I didn't hear a sound

It seems I have lost my smile
The way I used to sing
The sun doesn't shine as bright anymore
Without my Popcorn King

When Popcorn died on the road that day
Something in me died as well
I loved him so much
If he was alive that would be swell

People say life must go on
But life won't be the same
I'll never forget him for eternity
Life when it's gone is such a shame.

Emma King (13)
Alderley Edge School for Girls

Crab, Reindeer And Sleep

Sleep is a friend
Cast a spell to get rid of sleep
You're a total zombie
You twist and turn and
Exchange sides of your bed
Dream about a deep blue sea
Though it's brown and muddy
Sea can be cold
And your feet go numb
Crabs pinch but you eat them for revenge
Bake them in seawater
And the crab becomes salty
Tastes horrible
Reindeer once roamed free like the crab
Though crab offended
You prefer to eat the reindeer
Sounds weird and unfair
Speaking secret languages is a crime
Jealousy can make you learn a whole new language
Same language as the crab and reindeer
Respect those you wish to learn from
The French can speak French
And the Spanish, Spanish so
Let your hands get covered in ink
Because the ink was used to write your wisdom.

Amy Baston (12)
Alderley Edge School for Girls

This Is A Poem

This is a poem,
As you can see,
Its rhyming scheme is
AB, CB.

This verse has a simile,
Written by me,
It is meaningful and powerful,
Like the roaring sea

And this verse has a proper noun,
Full of awesome power,
It is very big and bold,
Like the Eiffel Tower.

Very vexed and verified verse,
Sitting in a station,
Perplexed, pompous, unpleasant,
Full of approximately accurate alliteration.

This poem finishes at the end of this verse,
Just like it started at the start,
It finishes with a question too,
Does it end with a question mark?

Joanna Lonsdale (12)
Alderley Edge School for Girls

Cats

Cats, cats, sleek and quick of foot
Some in white, some as black as soot
Cat flap, cat nap, coming in to sleep
Dreaming of field mice instead of sheep
Only getting up for food and play
This is their rota, day after day.

Emma Wigglesworth (12)
Alderley Edge School for Girls

Out In The Open

Washing, drying
Birds flying
In the breeze one day
Tree swishing
Men fishing
Out in the open way

Clouds floating
People joking
And kids just play, play, play
Blue skies
Green eyes
All out in the open.

Caroline Hopkins (11)
All Saints Catholic College

You

If fast or slow,
If you can throw high or low,
You are you.

If brainy or kind,
If a sweet or soft mind,
You are you.

If funny or pretty,
If you like puppies or kitties,
You are you.

If musical or a bookworm,
If you like to shout or squirm,
You are you.

Jodie Brown (11)
All Saints Catholic College

Winter

Winter has almost come upon us
The dark, damp evenings are nearly here
Scarves and hats come out of the drawer
As snow, rain and sleet draw near

Salt appears in buckets
As ice freezes on streets
Christmas trees are decorated
With yummy chocolate treats

Before we know it though Christmas passes
At the end of a cold December
As a new year starts
We'll sit back and remember.

Amelia Cowburn (12)
All Saints Catholic College

A Black Cat At Night

A black cat at night
Is like a black shadow
It sprints like an athlete
Trying for gold

The black cat creeps
Like a burglar at night
Its eyes are like marbles
When the headlights shine on them

The black cat hunts in silence
Like a fisherman catching his prey.

Adam Noble (13)
All Saints Catholic College

You Are My Hero

You are my hero
And you'll always be
The most important
Person to me

You're always there
When I'm sad
To help me through
When things seem bad

You care for me
All day through
When there are lots
Of things to do

I love you Mum
For all you do
For loving me
And my sisters too

You are my hero
And you'll always be
The most important
Person to me.

Lucy Taylor (13)
All Saints Catholic College

Sight

Sound, taste, smell and touch
Are the best things in my life.
There's only one thing in my life
That I'd trade these for . . .
Sight!
I'd love to see light and the wonders of the night,
My mum and dad tell me of the wonders that must be,
Oh I'd love to just take one look at a tree,
The one thing I'd love to do
Would be to be able to see!

Thomas Bailey (13)
All Saints Catholic College

Animal Poetry

Cheetah, cheetah, cheetah
Fearful animal of the night
Prowling
Cheetah, look how you cheat
Faster than lightning,
How could you get more frightening?
You sleep in the day, you sleep in the night,
You sleep when you feel it's right.
You're a wild, fearful, prowling animal of the night,
Stalking its prey, getting ready to pounce.

Cheetah, cheetah, cheetah,
Faster than lightning,
Ready to pounce,
How much more can you ask for?

When you run, it's a whizzing sound,
Running through trees that go crack and pop,
Rivers that splash and fall.

Adam Wharmby (13)
All Saints Catholic College

The Dragon

A fire-breathing menace,
Flying, flying by, flying high.
A fire-breathing menace,
Some say they're mystical,
Some say they're beautiful.
Dragons live in caves,
Dragons live in raves,
Some live in castles
And some are little rascals.
The fire-breathing god and goddesses,
Lurking throughout the forests.

Shaun O'Neill (13)
All Saints Catholic College

My First Day At School

My first day at school
I started to cry very bad
I really was sad

They forced you to sleep
At least a few hours a day
It was so boring

I'm in the toy house
What can we have for dinner?
Maybe fish fingers

Is it time to read?
I like reading Biff and Chip
Please can we read now?

Do we have to work?
Now what do we have to do?
What is 2+2?

Now we are painting
No, I haven't done it right
Now it is perfect

It is dinner time
I'm hungry, I need to eat
What do we do next?

It is now home time
'Get your bag and coats everyone'
Says the teacher there.

Scott Wadsworth (11)
All Saints Catholic College

Topsy-Turvy

In my world everything is topsy-turvy
The mice go *frrr*
The cat goes *woof* and the people
Say all kinds of stuff
You sit on the cooker
You sleep in the bath
Sleeping on the toilet can be a barrel of laughs
You can go to school at weekends
And the homework pile never ends
I always wondered how life would be if
Everything wasn't topsy-turvy.

Christine Cooper (12)
All Saints Catholic College

What If . . .

What if life is less than what we thought?
What if life can't be store bought?
What if life is what we make it?
What if we have to go beyond the limit . . .
Will we take the chance and make our lives wonderful
Or leave and remain forever ponderful?
Maybe life is none of these
Or maybe life is here to please.
However you make it, bad or good,
Life will be the way it should.

Kirsty-Leanne Charlesworth (13)
All Saints Catholic College

King Arthur's Epitaph

King Arthur was a fearless knight
Who needed twenty scribes to write
The letters that he wanted wrote
To pass across the moat
Of the castle he was besieging
To add to his growing region
Gaining knights and fighting battles
Farming land and herding cattle
Married the fair Guinevere
Whose friendly smile stretched ear to ear
He had a castle at Camelot
Where all his knights like Lancelot
Feasted and had tournaments
Waiting for news behind battlements
And when came enemy invaders
They went out to stop the raiders
All rebellions were dissolved
And all the troubles were resolved
Sadly this reign came to an end
A tragedy was round the bend
His nephew started to rebel
So Arthur's army beat him as well
Sadly Arthur himself was slain
And that's the end of his fine reign.

David Williams (12)
Altrincham Grammar School for Boys

Twice Upon A Time I Saw . . .

One official oxtail overloading,
Two tall tintinnabulations talking,
Three thundering thumbs threshing,
Four fiery fries frothing,
Five furious figs frying,
Six sorted Scots sewing,
Seven slippery songs sailing,
Eight exhausted eggs evolving,
Nine noted nomenclatures nipping,
Ten tense teachers tackling,
Eleven elastic elephants eating,
Twelve tall turtles tinkering,
Thirteen tangled tangerines tormenting,
Fourteen fat fingers folding,
Fifteen furious flags fighting.

Alex Stewart (11)
Altrincham Grammar School for Boys

Owl

Silent is the owl
Whilst it captures its prey
Out by nightfall
Hidden by day

Invisible is the owl
When hooting its howl
Wandering alone
On its prowl

Giant is the owl
As it spreads its wings
Flying past the moon
Above everything.

Joel McLoughlin (11)
Altrincham Grammar School for Boys

The Two Seas

The roaring waves smashing on the rocks,
The howling wind blowing through my hair,
The driftwood hurled onto the beach,
Like a broken toy.

Abandoned fishing boats lying in the bay,
Being tossed up and down by a huge monster,
The white spray blowing up
And nothing left to see.

Suddenly, everything is quiet,
The monster lying down, purring like a cat
And everything is calm,
As people flood onto the sand.

Children playing, splashing,
Wading in the shallows,
Building with the sand,
Next to the sea.

Philip Marchant (12)
Altrincham Grammar School for Boys

Front Line

In the cold, dark night,
The troops are marching,
Towards the place they will fight

They set up camp,
'It's going to be a long night,' they say,
They lie on the floor that is cold and damp.

The next day, out of the bed they jerk,
Wishing they were home,
Into the trees where the enemy spies lurk.

The sound of breathing,
It seems to get harder each step,
Every troop knows they might not be leaving.

Christian Sadler (11)
Altrincham Grammar School for Boys

A School Day

I wake up in the morning
And I always wake up yawning
My alarm clock ringing
And the songbirds singing
I have my toasted bun
In the morning sun
Get dressed for school
Which I believe is cruel
As I wish to lie in, in the morning

When I get to my class
I wish I could give it a pass
But I have to be there
Or I'll have to pay the fare
By the end of the day
I'm worn away
And I feel like going to sleep
But I've homework to do
And it's stuck to me like glue
And it'll never go away

When it's time for bed
I rest my head
And I begin to fall asleep.

Joe Hesford (11)
Altrincham Grammar School for Boys

Hurricane Andrew

They know it's coming
Twenty-four hours
Frantic search
Photographs, jewellery, bank books, passports, blankets
Torches, food, water, clothes and shoes
Wind picking up outside
Garage doors banging, close the shutters
Keep the radio on for news

It's time, 3am, down to the basement
A strange calm descends
Then the wind roars
They curl up in their blankets
Hoping it will be alright
There's scraping as the hurricane sweeps up objects
And takes them along with it
Now the sound deadens, the hurricane is moving on
It is now safe
Roofs have been peeled away
Exposing wet pinkish plywood joints
Telephone poles snapped in two
Trees uprooted strewn across the highway
Flood waters ebb away.

Andrew Veitch (12)
Altrincham Grammar School for Boys

David Beckham

David Beckham MBE,
Drove his Ferrari into a tree!
The ambulance came and Brooklyn survived,
But poor old David said nothing and died.

The funeral arrived
And everybody cried,
For the big, lavish service was full of memories,
But the 5 million fans got to Madrid with ease.

Matthew Walley (11)
Altrincham Grammar School for Boys

My Autobiography

Born in Hexham in Northumberland,
On January 21st 1991.
Two big sisters and a dad and mum
And a pet called Bonny.
Moved to Hale when I was one,
Started nursery when I was three.
Also wanted to be an ice cream man,
But now I think that is silly.
When I started primary school at four,
Made lots of friends who wouldn't call me names.
We started going to Abersoch,
When I got bitten by a dog,
Wouldn't touch another dog after that.
When I told my friends I got bitten by a dog,
They all laughed.
Been at school for seven years
Before I knew it, I was doing the 11+,
I passed it by far.
Then I had a choice of school,
So I picked Altrincham School for Boys,
I started Altrincham Grammar for Boys
And made lots of friends.
Thank goodness because I couldn't have wished for better.
Found the work hard,
But finally got there.
Finally started Year 8 with a new attitude,
I wouldn't dream of being an ice cream man now,
I want to be a pilot
And hopefully it will be a success.
I am in the middle of Year 8 now
And going to give it all my weight.

James Favas (12)
Altrincham Grammar School for Boys

Autobiographical Poem

Today is the day
Where for once I do something educational
Where I sit down and write if I may
For you something oh so sensational

One day when I was small
Went to a museum loaded with fun
Got trapped in a lift so tall
My parents, boy did they run

Another time in Wales
My friends they ran down a hill
I fell into a big patch of nettles
Now with running, I get a chill

It was a windy day at the beach
I took a pram for a run down the sand
I let go to give Mummy a speech
And boy, did the pram have a band

It was a windy day up north
Little me and my dad took a walk
The strong wind nearly took me up forth
But Dad got me like a fork

When I was only about one or two
I went to a sailing club, I walked the jetty
I slipped and fell into the blue
But Dad jumped in after to get me!

My name is Sammy Rogers
I'm a fun, loveable guy
I like to eat jammy dodgers
But I'm not too keen on pie.

Sam Rogers (12)
Altrincham Grammar School for Boys

Autobiographical Poem

When I was just so very young,
On the golf course by a nettle I was stung,
Golf balls my dad would seek and find,
To throw in front of my small mind,
All excited I would run
And shout, 'Look, there's one!'
Never knowing what he'd really done.

When I was just four years old,
On my birthday I was told,
To blow out the candles, one, two, three,
Except someone blew them out for me,
I was so upset and I wanted to cry,
We re-lit the candles,
When everyone had said goodbye.

I once stupidly climbed over a fence,
I must have lost all my sense,
I made it over very safely,
But on the way back I slipped
And ripped my leg open rather nastily,
I staggered forward and gave a great moan,
In result I had to be carried home.

Carl Vernon (12)
Altrincham Grammar School for Boys

Memories

Going to the party, present in my hand
Buying drinks of Coca-Cola
Jumping into the rainbow ball pit
Getting stuck in the tunnels
Pass the parcel and musical bumps
Playing all day and eating cake

Playing on the swing, sweet in my mouth
Falling to the ground
Getting scared as I looked at my badly broken arm
Lying in uncomfortable hospital beds
Toast and jam in the morning with get well cards
My birthday in hospital, my arm in a cast
All these memories rushing through my head
This remembering makes me tired, I think I'll go to bed . . .

Tim Evans (12)
Altrincham Grammar School for Boys

Nightfall

As night falls
Upon the town
A person removes their
Dressing gown,
As night falls
The sun is setting,
All is ended,
Soft snoring,
As night falls
It's nearly midnight,
All around
There is no light,
As night falls
It is wrong
To say
As it is the new day.

Henry Brown (11)
Altrincham Grammar School for Boys

Memories

Oh look at all the memories,
Oh look at all the fun.

The first thing I remember was down at Jungle Jim's,
I sat on a slide which was made to look like a snake with powerful fins.

I sat there small and weak and wanted to go down,
But I was scared to meet the terrible laughing clown.

Oh look at the memories,
Oh look at the fun.

I remember my first dream
And I was part of a team.

During my relaxing kip,
I was standing on the deck of a pirate ship.

I ran across and then climbed up
And then I realised I was in a shape like a giant tea cup.

I looked around
And then fell to the ground.

Oh look at all the memories,
Oh look at all the fun.

I remember moving house,
With all the builders thinking I was a louse.

I made pet dinosaurs using wood,
I found these turned out very good.

I remember moving day,
I remember wanting to play.

I remember climbing up the ladder which was pretty wrong,
It was very tall and long.

Oh look at the memories,
Oh look at the fun.

Daniel Melling (12)
Altrincham Grammar School for Boys

I Remember!

I remember collecting football stickers with my brothers,
Beckham was the best in the whole album.

I remember that happy night when my brother was born,
I was waiting at home with my aunt.

I remember playing 'Warhammer' with my younger brother,
He started chewing a soldier then choked on his head.

I remember bashing my head on a rock and blood was everywhere,
My mum and dad then took me to the hospital where I recovered.

I remember getting stuck in the middle of a slide,
I was very upset and scared.

I remember on Christmas night seeing Santa Claus,
It was really my dad in disguise.

I remember my first day in primary school,
I didn't let my dad go home and I held his hand very tight.

I remember running at full pace straight into a glass door,
Luckily it did not smash (but I was in pain).

I remember one summer in Canada, capsizing in a canoe
with my cousin,
My brother came to the rescue in a powerboat he had
never driven before.

I remember great holidays with my family and friends,
Skiing in Scotland was fantastic.

I remember making new friends when I joined AGSB,
It was a big step in my life.

I will keep making more big steps in life with my family,
Going further and further . . .

Remembering more and more . . .

Jonathan Faupel (12)
Altrincham Grammar School for Boys

The Farmer, The Hen And The Fox

The wind blows
The cock crows
All this in Mr Parm's country farm

The frightened hens begin to flee
As the fox eyes with glee
The farmer watches with his gun
As the brutal deed waits to be done

The farmer creeps out
And gives an almighty shout
Startled birds and animals sense danger
For this is no friendly wildlife ranger

Darting eyes and pricked-up ears
The fox is alive to all his fears
Farmer lifts his gun and takes aim
And for the fox, this turns to a deadly game.

Dominic Bates (11)
Altrincham Grammar School for Boys

Sunshine

The sun is shining in the sky,
The flowers love it, so do I.
When it shines,
It sends a prickle down my spine.
It rules the sky with its rays,
It shines all through the day.
Until the night when the moon comes out,
The sun has to wait until the moon blacks out.
Then the sun jumps out from the east,
Oh, it's such a beautiful beast.
Rising in the east and setting in the west,
The sun's the best.

Alex Cusick (12)
Altrincham Grammar School for Boys

The Life Of A Leaf

A leaf hung down from a tree
And said, 'Dude, look up at me,
I'm not very old,
But I'll grow big and bold
And I'm still young, green and free.'

The leaf was hot in the sun
And said, 'Hey, I'm having fun,
The air is so clean
And my face is still green,
But it's not long till autumn.'

The leaf was changing colour
And said, 'I'm looking duller,
I don't like this red,
I haven't been fed
And the wind is getting fuller.'

The leaf lay flat on the ground,
But made not a single sound,
His face was all worn,
All shrivelled and torn,
With snow all gathered around.

Tom Cottrell (11)
Altrincham Grammar School for Boys

The Tiger

A striped fur coat flicks through the trees,
Sounds of heavy breathing come through the bushes,
The animal doesn't realise until it's too late,
The predator pounces and the animal is slain,
Life and death in the fast lane.

Philip Conti-Ramsden (11)
Altrincham Grammar School for Boys

Night Fox

The sun is low and a warm glowing red
The people are at home and are going to bed
The night crawls nearer, it is getting dark
The moon is in the sky, a shining silver arc
What's that? A shadow on the wall
Now it's gone like nothing was there at all
There it is again, two glinting green eyes
Just like two stars, sparkling in the skies
The crash of a falling pail
A glimpse of a reddish bushy tail
The barn owl's cries
Are silenced by the sight of those glinting green eyes
There's a scurry of claws
Now a creaking of doors
There's a flapping of wings
A morn cockerel sings
There's dew on the lawn
It's coming to morn
Another hen
Has been taken from its pen

The night fox must fly!

Alex Barker (11)
Altrincham Grammar School for Boys

Ugh! School

The sun outside is shining so bright,
But with my school books I have to fight,
I try to read about ancient Rome and its fall,
But I'd lots rather be out playing ball.

Just to be out there with glove in hand
And to make a double would be grand,
But alas! Here I sit with spelling and maths,
This school day seems to last and last.

I dream of hitting a long home run,
Bringing in the winning run, it would be fun,
But then the teacher interrupts, 'What is two and four?'
I can't think of anything but a baseball score.

But hark! What is that I now hear?
A shuffle of feet, the time is near,
There it goes, the ringing of the bell,
The school day is over, isn't it swell!

Michael Booth (11)
Altrincham Grammar School for Boys

The Man In The Park

Mr Jones was sitting in the park one day,
It was in the spring around April or May.
He shouted at the children as they ran by,
'You kids today, my oh my!
You're always charging here and there,
You don't give a thought, you don't even care.
Your hair is a shambles, your clothes are a joke!'
But the children just laughed as the old man spoke.
Deep in his memory something stirred,
Thoughts of his childhood free as a bird.
Riding on bikes, rushing down lanes,
So much excitement, so many games.
Then time as a soldier, gallant and fair,
Fighting for freedom, abroad, over there
And then in the churchyard, the sound of bells ringing
And all around people merrily singing.
Life as a husband with sons of my own,
Memories so real, but now so alone.
One thing's for certain, this comes to us all,
The tall and the mighty, the big and the small.
Don't just see the wrinkles, the lines, the grey hair,
Look closer at *me,* the man who sits there.

Michael Shaw (12)
Altrincham Grammar School for Boys

The First Day Of Term

The blazer is on, the tie is up,
My mates turn round and say, 'What's up?'
I say, 'Nothing' but I know I've lied,
As I look nervously from side to side.

I hear footsteps down the corridor,
There was silence, then uproar,
Cheering, laughing and mocking too,
Where was this coming from? Was it the loo?

Through the door I went outside,
Then I saw something that made me hide,
A boy hanging another boy above a bin,
This was not right, it must be a sin.

I hear the bell ringing loud,
I retreat to the form room without a sound,
I sit down just in time,
Just in time to finish this rhyme.

Hedayat Javidi (12)
Altrincham Grammar School for Boys

Beautiful Sounds

The sound of brown, fallen leaves crunching as you step on them,
The trees swooshing in the midsummer breeze out in a
large, open field,
Birds chirping up in the pale blue sky, with not a cloud in sight,
I hear cows in the next field,
A river flowing, cascading downstream,
Running through a rough grass field
Makes my legs tingle, with the wind brushing your face –
That's when you know you're free.

Byrone Heywood (12)
Coppenhall High School

Myself

My name is Carl Plant,
All I ever do is rant.
I am a short little Brummie,
With a small tummy.
But don't mess with me
Or I'll wrap you round the tree.
I've got dark hair
And a head shaped like a pear.
I've got long legs
And feet like pegs.
My arms are big,
With fingers like twigs.
I've got small blue eyes,
But shaped like pies.
I've got a nose,
As long as a hose.
I live in a house,
With a massive great mouse.
I love my mummy,
She puts food in my tummy.

Carl Plant
Coppenhall High School

The Wind

Stepping out of my door
I feel the wind blow
It's like the roar of a lion
Or a squeak of a mouse

The wind is loud as it whistles by
Picking up rubbish, floating high in the sky
As it hurries on; picking up speed

The wind can be your friend by helping you sail
The wind can be your foe when it is blowing a gale
Leaving you frozen, clinging to a rail.

Laura Rowley (11)
Coppenhall High School

My Cat

I have a cat called Stumpy,
His fur is black and white.
When he's inside he sleeps all day,
But wanders in the night.

If he doesn't get what he wants,
He tends to go in a mood.
So we try to please him,
By giving him some food.

My cat likes to go hunting,
He goes and hunts for mice.
When they move, he pounces on them,
Which isn't very nice.

I'll always love my cat
And I always will do,
But I'm sure if you saw him,
You would love him too.

Sarajane Passey (11)
Coppenhall High School

British Sporting Pride

My favourite team is Man U,
The worst team play in blue.
I enjoy watching the British Lions,
While on my face it's covered in smiles.

During the winter, the best thing's cricket,
I enjoy watching the bowler hit the wickets.
The ball can take a large bounce,
The fielder watches the ball till he can pounce.

Although they never seem to win,
The cricket team get in.
In a match of hockey,
They always seem to get cocky.

Jamie Dutton (12)
Coppenhall High School

Christmas Time

Christmas is a time of cheer
A wonderful atmosphere
Laughing, dancing
Round the tree
Everybody full of glee
Presents all over the floor
Santa's bringing even more
It's Christmas Eve, calm and quiet
Next door is having a riot
Now it's peaceful and calm
I have to set my alarm
Now off to bed it is for me
Because in the morning there will be presents under the tree
Now it's morning, I have begun
To open my presents, oh what fun
After dinner, I will see what dessert is in for me
Look through the window of the kitchen
There is my dessert next to the chicken
I thank you for reading my poem
But now I am going to turn off the fire, my cheeks are glowing.

Hayley Maginnis (15)
Coppenhall High School

I Am . . .

I am a speeding limousine going down the M6 motorway
Or a bike leaning against a broken fence.

I am a rainbow sparkling all my colours
Or rain pouring to the ground.

I am a waterfall hiding in a cave
Or weak tree breaking branches off.

I am a proud cheetah looking around at my cubs
Or a black and white puppy shivering in its kennel.

Ben Harrop (12)
Coppenhall High School

Here To Stay!

We are aliens and we're here to stay!
Everybody does know who we are,
We hang around in crowds,
Freak people out,
Just because we have:
Round, tiny, dark purple bodies,
With square heads and overgrown eyes,
We eat anything people give us,
Go around destroying everything,
Houses, buildings, shops,
People get scared!
Shouting and screaming,
We don't eat humans,
It's only because
We are aliens and here to stay!

Claire Pettitt (13)
Coppenhall High School

I Am . . .

I am a silver jet plane speeding in the air
Or an old bi-plane lying in a scrap heap.

I am a heatwave going around the world
Or a hurricane spinning in the field.

I am the sea going fast to the sand
Or a rusty, old steam train puffing out black smoke.

I am a cheetah running to catch my prey
Or a turtle going slowly into the sea.

I am a rock star rocking the street
Or a Goth singing loud.

I am Disneyland in Florida having fun with all the kids
Or a hut made out of hay burning down.

David Bennion (12)
Coppenhall High School

The Sky

The star shone bright
In the middle of the night

When it comes out
The sun goes away
And millions of stars come out to play

They bounce around
While we watch on the ground

Some are dying,
While we are spying,
Through a telescope.

Astronauts hope
They can find a new planet to study,
But they will have to hurry.

Mark Triner (13)
Coppenhall High School

The Haunted House Rap

I walked into a haunted place,
There was nothing there but a skeleton case.
There were bones and guts,
Bruises and cuts.
There suddenly became a terrible noise,
It was only a baby playing with toys.

But where did this baby come from?
Wait a minute, where's it gone?
It might be a ghost, we'll never know,
Where the heck did it go?

This is a problem we'll never solve,
We just don't know whom to involve.
So listen here, I got something to say . . .
We don't find the baby, you're gonna *pay!*

Jessica Heath (12)
Coppenhall High School

Harry Potter's Star Scar

Scar, scar,
Burning, burning,
Harry Potter, yearning, yearning.

Voldemort, Voldemort, You Know Who!
Wicked, evil and powerful too.

Someone help -
Hear his pain,
Harry's scar is burning again!

Once he was thought to have been dead,
All because of the scar on his forehead.

Scar, scar,
Burning, burning,
Harry Potter no longer yearning.

He's found fame!
He's found friends!
Harry Potter is brave, courageous and a wizard no longer the same.

Now he's a star,
Thanks to Voldemort,
Hogwarts and his
Scar.

Emily Bennett (12)
Coppenhall High School

Fear On A Deserted Island

F rightened, deserted, I'm all alone
E vening comes and I'm getting cold
A nxiously my eyes are closing
R oaring thunder wakes me up.

Kowser Ahmed (12)
Coppenhall High School

The Thunderstorm Is . . .

A destructive beast
A threatening flash
An elephant stampede
A tiger's killer claw
A murdering black sheep
A demolition giant
A jet-black blanket in the sky
A hammering downpour
An everyday nightmare
An electric shock
A deafening lion
A splitting horror
A moaning cloud.

Thomas Butters (11)
Coppenhall High School

The Thunderstorm Is . . .

The thunderstorm is . . .
A destructive flash
An electric light
A deafening roar
A child's dread
A howling wolf
A patter on the roof
A stampede racing around
A bad day's weather
A split cloud.

Matthew Hallyburton (11)
Coppenhall High School

Journey To Hogwarts

There it stood, gleaming like a ruby over the bustling crowds,
Awaiting for students to flood into its carriages,
We hear hooting like an owl,
This can only mean one thing -
Students rush to their seats,
Running down the tracks like a roadrunner
Hunting for the immaculate school
Passing the beauty of the countryside
It turns dark
It starts to slow down
The journey is ending
Suddenly it stands to a slow halt
Students flee off the amazing transport
They have arrived
Faces looking dull and gloomy as the journey is over.

Abigail Burrow (11)
Coppenhall High School

Island

S ince I've been on this island, it's been a struggle,
T he first day was like Hell for me,
R eally, really scared when I could not find any other survivors,
A nd I was very hungry,
N othing could make me stop looking for food,
D eath felt near for me,
E ventually I found some food,
D eath was now not so close.

Joe Gardiner (11)
Coppenhall High School

War

How would you feel
If you were out on the battlefield,
No one there to help you,
Nothing as your shield,
Bombs falling, guns firing,
Bodies at your feet?
The men whom you've just met
Or those you have yet to meet
The innocent blood running down
The faces of the dead
Forest leaves underneath them
Acting as their bed
The lovers of the perished men
Will soon be drowning in their tears
In this forest soon, as the darkness nears.

Ben Grice (12)
Coppenhall High School

The Island

D eserted on an island
I n fear of hunger
S taring out over the sea to seek a sign of a ship
T rying to stay alive on salty water and fruit
R aring to go home and see my family
A lways on my mind, the thought of lives lost
U nconscious on the sandy shore
G oing slowly, but not in pain
H urting, nothing or no one to help me
T ender, sore, help wanted desperately.

Samantha Cartwright (11)
Coppenhall High School

Cattle-Bery

Cattle-bery, oh Cattle-bery your eyes are bright,
In the night,
Reflecting the light.

Cattle-bery, oh Cattle-bery your fur is black,
Upon your back,
Like a haystack.

Cattle-bery, oh Cattle-bery your tail goes swish,
Just as you
Catch a fish.

Cattle-bery, oh Cattle-bery you always seek,
With your tiny little feet,
For fresh cooked meat.

Cattle-bery, oh Cattle-bery you are so furry
And so nice,
Just like a McFlurry ice.

Cattle-bery, oh Cattle-bery you are so sweet,
I love to see
Your tiny little feet.

Cattle-bery, oh Cattle-bery I love you so
And I am never
Going to let you go!

Sam Cormack (12)
Coppenhall High School

The Island

I am stranded on an island
S taring out across the sea
L onely and isolated from the rest of the world
A ngry and cold
N eed to go home
D esperately.

Julian Powell (11)
Coppenhall High School

Hedwig's Flight

I sit quietly on my perch, waiting for a job.
I hear my name being called and soar into the night.
In the Hogwarts grounds I meet McGonagall and Wood,
They give me a package and I start an early flight.
I fly over the Forbidden Forest and the sea,
As I flew over the water, a mermaid gave me a fright.
I carried on flying and rest on an oak tree,
From there I kept on flying and the wind didn't half bite!
I wondered what I was carrying, so I stopped to see.
It was in a peculiar shape and with all my might,
I opened the package to find a broomstick for Harry.
I quickly re-wrapped the broomstick and flew off like a kite.
I had to fly quickly if I wanted to get back.
I was nearly there now, Hogwarts was in sight,
I had to keep going because breakfast would be soon.
I made it into the great hall just as it became light.
I was thanked for the delivery and went to sleep,
Back on my perch in the owlery, I dreamt of my flight.

Rhys Ingham (11)
Coppenhall High School

The Wind Is . . .

A scary whistle
A lion's roar
A person's scream
A tree swaying
A snake's rattle
A flower shocked
A leaf falling
A terrified family
A bird's tweet
The laughter of a child.

Stephanie Clayton (11)
Coppenhall High School

The Hogwarts Express

It's come to that time of year again,
When we all must catch the Hogwarts train.
Laughing and chatting with all our friends,
As the train takes us whizzing around the bends.
Chocolate frogs and cauldron cakes,
To quash our hunger is what it takes.
As we all look out and up at the moon,
We all know we'll be there soon.
There is excitement and anticipation,
As the train pulls up at Hogsmeade Station.

Stuffing our pockets with all our sweets,
All waiting on the edge of our seats.
Everyone's smiles are back on their faces,
when they spot Neville tripping over his laces.
It's time for us all to go change into our gowns,
Because the Hogwarts Express is slowing down.

Leanne Chesters (12)
Coppenhall High School

Island

I am stranded, washed upon the shore
S ilent, still and deserted
L ooking for help from ships
A nd not giving up
N ow ready to explore the deserted island
D angerous it will be, but I will take the risk.

Ashley Scoffin
Coppenhall High School

Mansion Fever

Out in the darkness the eagle takes flight,
Above the mansion it's an eerie sight,
To the mansion in the main hall,
Nothing is moving, nothing at all.

A mist hangs around the place hidden in the air,
That long ago banished all sense of fair,
Something went on here but nobody knows,
There are no survivors to hear rumours be told.

Crimson blood stains the corridor walls,
In all the rooms including the halls,
The worries inside me I can barely contain,
I think I'm going crazy I need a restraint.

The forsaken laboratories are no longer used,
All the rusty elevators have all blown their fuse,
The specimens here look decayed but not dead,
If they ever were alive we'd all lose our head.

I ran from that place as fast as I could,
But I didn't survive, nobody would,
Once they knew the secret that this mansion bore,
No one will live, not one will stand tall.

Chris Halford (12)
Coppenhall High School

The Dark Is . . .

The dark is . . .
A quilt of black
A walking nightmare
A fierce tiger
Striking lightning
Packs of wolves howling
People screeching
A black panther
Darkness.

Anthony Jamhour (11)
Coppenhall High School

Alien Friend!

Aliens are from different planets,
We call it outer space,
They travel in big UFOs
And want to take over the human race

They live on planet Mars
And work day in, day out
On Mars they have the greatest bars
And drink beer with their snouts

These aliens don't have any friends
Because of their strict boss
They are not allowed any trends
Because this man is very cross

If I lived on this planet
I would have to change the rules
I would brush up all the granite
And stop them acting like fools.

Alexander David King (13)
Coppenhall High School

Abandoned On An Island

A bandoned on an island
B orn to be part of a family
A nd part of life
N ot a part of an island
D eath feels so near
O cean is all around me
N eglected by my family
E ating fruits and
D eserted, please help me.

Laura Rowlands (11)
Coppenhall High School

The Little Pussy Cats

Five little pussy cats
Sitting by the door
One saw a mouse
Then there were four

Four little pussy cats
Standing in a tree
One fell off
Then there were three

Three little pussy cats
Sitting in a queue
One saw a dog
Then there were two

Two little pussy cats
Sitting in the sun
One got burnt
Then there was one

One little pussy cat
His name was Rocky Ron
He went home
Then there were none.

Krystal Latham (13)
Coppenhall High School

The Island

D eserted on a tropical island
I n fear of hunger
S tarving and lonely
T hirsty and scared
R oaring with thunder and lightning
A nd desperate to escape
U nder the wood I lie
G asping without breath, saying 'Help'
H urt and disturbed
T he night goes, another day.

Matthew Bennett (11)
Coppenhall High School

What Would Aliens Do?

The shiny plate,
Which flies through space,
Inhabited by an alien race,
Passing through the pitch-black place,
At a high speedy rate.

Eight bright lights around the rim,
So the aliens know where they're going,
Passing over different planets,
Until they get to Earth.

One alien inside the ship,
Saw Earth and thought,
'Well, I quite like this!'

But the real question was,
What would the aliens do?
Would they decide to come in peace
Or invade us like evil beasts?

Sam Jamhour (14)
Coppenhall High School

Tropical Island

T ired and lonely
R esting in dark caves
O cean all around
P eaceful nights, all alone
I n darkness I sit
C oldness fills the air
A bandoned with my friends
L onely without family, on an island.

Chloe Critchlow (11)
Coppenhall High School

Space

Deep in space,
Where the aliens are,
There are small men driving tiny cars.
Looking from Earth at the tiny stars,
Make a wish as hard as you can,
Up there on Mars,
Aliens look back at us,
Thinking what strange creatures we are,
Pluto sits all alone,
Like a naughty child at the back of the class.

The sun shines brightly
In the day,
At night the moon comes out to play.
Up there are Mercury, Neptune and Mars
And other planets like coloured stars.

In bed at night,
Look at the stars outside,
Then go to sleep,
Dreams so sweet.

Frances Ryder (13)
Coppenhall High School

The Sand Is . . .

The sand is a block of soft rubble,
The sand is a lock of silky blonde hair,
The sand is a stretch of white melted chocolate,
The sand is a long sway of yellow carpet,
The sand is a scoop of vanilla ice cream
The sand is a cream fluffy cloud
The sand is a misty cool breeze floating
The sand is a thick, creamy milkshake
The sand is a flat snowy mountain.

Claire Baker (11)
Coppenhall High School

Quidditch

Both houses walk onto the pitch,
Ready to start our match.
What I need is the Snitch,
That's what I need to catch.

Other team players pass,
As I shake with fear.
My feet skim the grass,
While the crowd cheer.

I'm flying everywhere,
So I clench my broom tight.
I glide through the air,
As day turns into night.

Sharna Gallagher (11)
Coppenhall High School

The Bird

The bird soars grandly though the sky,
Amazingly straight, straight as a die.

Its wings flap up and down,
Oh how perfectly they move, they make me frown.

Birds are such beautiful things,
I wish I were a bird,
When I see a bird so free,
They make my heart twing.

I wish I were a bird,
I wouldn't moan a word.

Christopher Wilcock (12)
Coppenhall High School

The Thing

There is an alien in town,
Who always sits near the pub, Crown.

When someone walks past,
The people stare in fright.

People say they have spoken to the alien
And all the alien says is 'Zalien.'

He looks like a giant piece of green jelly,
With three arms, three legs and a fat belly.

On its green face,
It has eyes all over the place.

His eyes are blue and red
And he's got a massive green head.

He looks around two foot two
And people say he should be in a zoo.

Will this alien go away?
And if he does, will anyone say hooray?

Chris Hulme (13)
Coppenhall High School

Oh! To Play For United

Oh, how I wish I was playing for United,
Crowds singing their hearts out to me,
I wish these dreams, I dream, could really be.

How I long to play in the theatre of dreams,
But it's a long way away, it seems.
Unless one day I could just be scouted,
Posters of me gilded and mounted.

But at the moment, I'm just stuck with dreams
And my posters on my wall,
Of players, coaches and managers,
Who have already dreamed it all.

Tom Darby (12)
Coppenhall High School

The Day The World Came To An End

People were flocking for cover

A person falling, then another.

Life was quickly fading

Shops were closing and speedily trading.

People laying in the roads

Pet shop quickly losing toads.

The moon left crumbled in the sky

Everyone started to wonder why.

People's limbs did this thing sever

They thought it would go on forever.

Finally the horror subsided

Though it left streets cluttered and untidied.

Benjamin Ollier (12)
Coppenhall High School

I Am . . .

I am a blue Jaguar cruising down the street
Or a rusty old Metro in a heap.

I am the wind slashing through the trees
Or the gentle snow falling in a silent street.

I am a sleek cheetah running along the riverside
Or a dirty, creepy dog digging in the street.

I am a speaker full with music
Or a dusty old radio with no batteries.

I am Jamaica doing a disco
Or a damp flat in Crewe, fast asleep.

Jamielee Challinor (12)
Coppenhall High School

Gymnastics

Gymnastics is fun and it keeps you fit,
You either like it a lot or just a bit,
You start with basics and work your way up
And when you're good enough, you'll win the cup,
When I go to work as hard as I can,
I get so hot, I turn on the fan,
I go into competitions and do my best
And when I've finished, I watch the rest,
My gym club is CNGC,
Come and join and you'll meet me,
When my day at gym is done,
I go home and meet my mum!

Sammie McGowan (12)
Coppenhall High School

Out Of Control And Under A Spell

Whizzing around, out of control,
Out of control and under a spell.
Hanging from one finger and toe,
Out of control and under a spell.
Flying up and down wondering what to do,
Out of control and under a spell.
Fall to the ground with the Snitch in his hand,
Out of control and under a spell.
Cheers fill the air from all around,
Out of control and under a spell.
Under a spell and out of control,
But still won the game!

Roxanne Mooney (11)
Coppenhall High School

Poo Poem

The thing that comes out of your rear end,
Maybe straight or curved in a bend,
It's not very nice and extremely smelly,
This is poo that's made in your belly.

Sometimes it's brown, sometimes it's green,
Purple is the worst I've ever seen,
Poo is wonderful, poo is great,
The most I've had in a day is eight.

I love poo,
It's totally the best,
Hip hip hooray, it's better than the rest.

Lauren May (11)
Coppenhall High School

Quivering Quidditch

Twirling round and round,
Trying hard not to look at the ground,
Dodging the Bludger,
Chasing the Snitch,
Make sure not to fall onto the pitch,
Slytherin is the team we have to beat,
I'll catch the Snitch, they'll admit defeat,
I'm the best there has ever been,
That's why they have chosen me for their team,
Harry Potter is my name
And Quidditch is my perfect game!

Sarah King-Evans (11)
Coppenhall High School

Ghost

Whilst walking up the corroded path,
I heard a murmur then a laugh,

When I looked all around,
No one was there to be found.

Then I stumbled upon the rock,
That was the key to the lock.

When the doors eventually unlocked,
The only thing I heard was the grandfather clock.

I took one step onto the floor,
When wood squeaked, it was like a lion's roar.

Suddenly bats came flying out,
So I gave an almighty shout.

I saw a ghost go whizzing past,
I heard the clock strike one at last.

A shiver of fear ran down my spine
And felt I was about to cross the death line.

The ghost kept with me all night,
Then I gave a black cat a fright.

It was sat on the edge of a four-poster bed
And was reading words from the book of the dead.

That night I was weary,
The night was eerie.

I knew this was my only chance,
To prove that people weren't in a trance.

I had the proof that I needed,
To show my mates, people weren't insane as they pleaded.

Natasha Vyse (13)
Coppenhall High School

Hogwarts Express

Steaming through the white cold frost,
Soaring down the track,
Turning a sharp corner,
Going into tunnels of black.

You never get bored of the journey,
The lady comes round with sweets,
There's a lot to look at out of the window,
While you eat a delicious treat.

The journey takes about an hour,
There isn't a big price to pay.
Just grab a seat on the Hogwarts Express
And you'll be on your way.

The steam is as hot as fire,
The track is as smooth as wood,
The tables are polished so shiny,
There is no sign of mud.

We are not very keen on animals,
They mess up the train you see,
So prove your pet is housetrained
And we will let it on for free!

Do not put fingers on the windows,
Do not put chewing gum on the seats,
Do not bring any dirt in
And always wipe your feet!

You might meet somebody famous,
We always have rich guests,
They always use our transport,
Because our train is the best!

That's our Hogwarts Express
Hogwarts Express is the best!

Natalie Williams (11)
Coppenhall High School

The Wind Is . . .

A lion's roar
A person's whistle
A person sneezing
A squiggly line
A white blanket spread across the land
An invisible line that you cannot see
A cloud drifting along the ground
A person's powerful push
A white ribbon being pulled along the sky
A sound of a child whistling
A blow of a hairdryer.

Emma Triner (11)
Coppenhall High School

I Am . . .

I am nice, kind and happy
Or I am sad and lonely
Except when I am with my friends
And then I am not lonely or on my own

I am the red Ferrari speeding down the motorway
Or the rusty, brown Reliant Robin waiting on the scrapheap

I am the heatwave passing over your house
Or Jack Frost scratching at your window

I am a red flower sitting in your garden
Or a dead plant in a big field.

Emma Giltrap (12)
Coppenhall High School

Britain

Britain is a fairly big place,
Full of smiles, with some disgrace,
The weather is never all that good,
As most people will have understood.

There are lots of attractions to go and see,
Alton Towers is the best one for me,
At Christmas there's too much shopping to do,
We exchange presents from me to you.

The seas are mostly black and grey,
As litter is thrown from day to day,
At football we're known for causing fights,
In the streets we're frustrated with all the traffic lights.

Sunday's the day we have a roast dinner,
My mum's are the best and always a winner.
There is loads to watch on TV,
You can sit and watch them with your family.

We're known for eating fish and chips,
In Cornwall 1999, I saw a total eclipse,
In cafés we buy cups of tea,
Chatting and nattering happily.

Tiffany McCann (12)
Coppenhall High School

All About . . .

A tiger's roar
A dangerous strike
Destroying everything in its path
A fiery light
A squiggly line
A destroying machine
People screaming.

Craig Minshull (11)
Coppenhall High School

Britain

The weather in Britain
Is such a shame
It's mostly wet
With plenty of rain

The food in Britain
Is very nice
It's warm and filling
And makes you feel good inside

Christmas is the best for me
With presents, trees and a warm cup of tea
Then we all have roast veg
And stuffing to go

Britain is friendly
But football can bring us disgrace

Britain is my home and place
I love Britain in every way!

Katie Bates (12)
Coppenhall High School

Lonely

L onely on a deserted island,
O nly yourself for company,
N ever seeing your friends or family,
E very place abandoned, wherever you go,
L ying on the sand all alone,
Y ou are scared.

Samantha Goodwin (11)
Coppenhall High School

The Fly Thing!

I woke up in the night
With a fright
I'd left on the landing light

And there it was, at the
Bottom of the stairs!
It was gross and had lots
Of ginger hairs

It had large googly eyes
Kind of like a giant fly

It had six tiny legs
And three very large heads
I quickly scrambled back into my bed

The fly thing flew right upstairs
Then I dared . . .
'Who are you and where are you from?'
'Nice meeting and greeting,' said the fly thing
And *poof* it was gone.

Jade O'Reilly (13)
Coppenhall High School

The Island Of Lost Dreams

M essage in a bottle
A ll I can do is wait
R uled out of the world
O ff to find my mates
O f all the unknown islands
N o one knows
E ating fruits and drinking from coconuts
D anger comes and goes.

Zach Chambers (11)
Coppenhall High School

Year 2050

The world will be different in the future,
But how?
Will there be flying cars, people living in space,
Aliens landing, coming to and fro?
But where will they come from?
Will people become supernatural
Like Batman or Robin?
Will UFOs be identified,
Is it just a fix?
Will there be a new dominant animal,
Or will it still be us?
Will you be able to go to school on the bus?
Will the war on terrorism be over?
Will there be world peace?
Will other planets be discovered?
With an atmosphere to support life
Nobody knows!

Christopher Dunn (13)
Coppenhall High School

The Island Of Despair

I stand tall and proud
S ea smashing against the cliff
L agoon shining bright and blue
A mazon thick and wild
N o-man's-land, dangerous and scary
D espair more and more.

Michael Ellis (11)
Coppenhall High School

Alien From Mars

A face like a football,
A torso like a brick wall,
Three arms like octopi tentacles,
Three legs like twigs.

The alien comes from Mars,
Bringing a disease called SARS,
The alien comes in a cylinder,
A big crash, straight through Crewe cinema.

I wonder if there are anymore aliens
Lying up there in Mars?
Humans are scared now, in case they get SARS.
The alien looks scared now,
Wouldn't you be if you were on your own?

Billy Clews (14)
Coppenhall High School

The Something Is . . .

A place where some people go,
A white glow in the air,
A priceless ship going up where the stars are above,
A white chocolate surface,
A rocky place in space,
A space of holes,
It stands out at night through the scope,
A place where a lot of people would dream to go.

Stephen Pietrusiak (11)
Coppenhall High School

It!

Who's the creature in the sea
That likes to watch and follow me?

With no footsteps in the sand
It has just one stumpy hand

It will sing along to your tunes
But will dance like a bunch of baboons

It isn't your ordinary playmate
But it isn't someone you can hate

It is a creature with no special feature

That just wants a pal
(Preferably a gal)

So please befriend *It*
And help *It* fit

Right into our place
Please just give *It* a friendly face.

Sally-Ann Pleavin (13)
Coppenhall High School

Quality Quidditch

Quality Quidditch broomsticks soar through the sky,
People staring watching them fly,
Players in a Quidditch match, fastest people there,
But they don't seem to care,
Because they're in mid-air.

Jemma Rowley (11)
Coppenhall High School

Untitled

We live in a universe full of planets
With some planets not yet discovered
You have Saturn with its beautiful rings
And Jupiter with its red eye
And the really cold and small planet, Pluto

I wonder if there are aliens somewhere out there?
I wonder if we will ever meet them?
Will they have five legs
And five arms
Or have thousands of squidgy eyes?
Will they have massive UFOs
With weapons that will kill us all
Or could they just be friendly?

James Webb (13)
Coppenhall High School

The Sun Is . . .

The sun is a fiery sphere
That has been fired
Into the sky by a cannon
A moon on fire
Evil's eyes
A secret bonfire with
Orange fireworks
A light to Earth
A small miracle.

Stephanie Jones (11)
Coppenhall High School

Aliens

Aliens seem to travel space
At an amazing pace,
It seems to be a race,
To get to a better place.

They step out of the UFO
And float down to say, 'Hello!'
Some are fat, some are thin,
Other bald, with transparent skin.

Do we stay and say hello
Or do we run and hide below?
Beneath the ground in shelters,
Deep; do not cry, do not weep.

Alien beings big and small,
They come to us because we call,
Out to space; to find a place
That we can call a home for all?

Aliens come from far and wide,
To see what people they can find,
Like us you see they don't know,
Where to stay and where to go.

To the moon or to the sun?
Is it hot? Could be fun
To find a place that's so neat,
Leafy green, like my street.

What's that I can hear?
Is it far? Is it near
No, it's Mum by my side,
'Get up girl, you'll be late,
Your Martian friend is at the gate.'

Rhianwen Haynes (13)
Coppenhall High School

My School Day

I went to school at half-past eight,
To make sure I was not late
I went to maths
Had some laughs
Later on I went to break
And I ate my Flake
Then to IT
To see what I could see
On the Internet I went
And saw a picture of a tent
English was now with a frown
Knowing I had to be a clown
Next came lunch with a smile
Knowing that I had a while
In tech
I'm up to my neck in all the work that's set
Next comes French
And I was ready to sit at my bench

Now the day is over
Now it's time to go
I pack my things away
Now I'm going home
Goodbye.

Stefan Phillips (12)
Coppenhall High School

All About Britain

In Britain the weather is bad
And nearly everyone turns very sad,
When the weather is hot,
The sun is like a big yellow dot.
On Sundays in Britain we have a roast,
At the seaside the shore hits from coast to coast,
Every morning we have a postman,
Driving his big red van.

Michaela Entwistle (12)
Coppenhall High School

Space And The Planets

'Welcome to the world of space'
UFOs flying
Meteoroids burning throughout space
Saturn spinning around and around
The moon is glowing nice and bright
The sun is sizzling at millions of degrees
How was the universe formed?
Why are we on planet Earth?
Rockets sent up from Earth
Mars the red burned planet
Uranus, the blue and green planet
Jupiter, the largest
Shooting stars whizzing
Comets shining
'Welcome to the world of space.'

Dan Sherratt (13)
Coppenhall High School

British Authors

In the truly brilliant Britain,
Many people have written,
Lots of books have been published
And many poems have been rubbished.
All day long people read and read,
Until they become to need and need.
More books are bought throughout the day,
People enjoy being at home to stay.
Books can be good, books can be boring,
You read them while pets are gnawing.

Steven Parker (12)
Coppenhall High School

Theme In Britain

In Britain there are lots and lots of shops,
You can buy some fancy tops,
You could cover yourself in jewels
And buy some fancy tools.

Every day there is bad weather,
You see people wearing heavy leather
And most of the time, day and night,
Through your window a flash of light.

Sometimes there are good soaps,
But there are some dopes,
EastEnders is the best,
From all the rest.

Bangers and mash,
Go well with potato hash
And with TV's Tango and Cash.

The very busy traffic light,
Changes to red, amber, green,
You might think the traffic is mean,
Oh! What a scene.

Jodie Grocott (12)
Coppenhall High School

The English Breakfast!

A plate is a big round world,
Sausages is the stick up trees,
Bacon is the patchy plots,
Tomatoes are the bushy leaves,
Hash browns are the houses with doors,
Egg is the glittering sun
And the white bit is the clouds pushing through the sky,
Fried bread is the slabs on the ground with cracks.

Melanie Challinor (12)
Coppenhall High School

All About Different Things In Britain

England is the place with bad weather
With some people that are clever
We have lots of rain
It is a pain
We have a good England team
When they score, we scream
We have great parks
You get big gangs in the dark
We have fish and chips on Friday
And roast dinners on Sundays
England's OK and quite fun
Especially when we get the sun
We have good fairs
That you can compare
So come over, if you dare.

Becky Cort (12)
Coppenhall High School

Come And Go

The aliens are coming,
falling from the sky,
ready to attack, but why?
They do what they want!
No one gets in their way,
but what they don't realise,
they can't come out in day.
So, when night falls,
all are hidden away,
because of the sun,
they have no fun.
Back they go into the sky,
everyone's asleep, so no one says bye!

Aimee Woolley (13)
Coppenhall High School

The Best British Player, Probably!

England's football team
Are the best,
Of course, better than the rest,
They score lots of goals,
Not hitting the poles.
David Beckham with his boots,
Kicking the ball as he hints,
Chewing on his minty mints.

At half-time,
They go for a drink,
Then have a wash in the sink.

They come out after half-time is over
Making sure they know
Where to go
And yet again another goal is scored
And everyone started to scream,
Whilst having their ice cream.

Emma Kennedy (12)
Coppenhall High School

My Home Town

Well, my home town
It's not very nice, it's not mostly
Crud weather, it's rainy day in, day out
Don't argue 'cause it is without a doubt
But when it is the summer
Our toes are not numb
But we are famous for some things
Like the railway station and
The Rolls Royce

Our footie team are all right
They could be better
I don't really support them, my mate does
Goodbye, this is my home town.

Adam Talbot (12)
Coppenhall High School

Things I Do On Sundays In Britain

England's Queen's Park is very good
Especially the swings,
You can go down to the lake
And feed the hungry swans.
When you run out of bread,
They chase you around and around,
So give up
And have a game of football,
If you get thirsty,
Have a Slush
Or go to the café
And have a tea.

Once you have done that,
Take a boat and go for a paddle,
If it wears your legs down,
Go and have a swing on the swings.

After a hard day's work,
Go home and watch TV,
Especially Corrie and EastEnders.

Danielle Reece (12)
Coppenhall High School

I Am . . .

I am the blue Lamborghini speeding down a road
Or the rusty silver Metro which is from a scrapheap.

I am a heatwave passing over steep hills
Or Jack Frost scratching at your window.

I am a buzzing bee flying around in an oak tree
Or I am a black cat walking down the road on a rainy day.

I am the loud drum beat of heavy rock
Or the harp with broken strings.

I am the big blue swimming pool
Or a dull street at night in the rain.

Jamie Mathieson (13)
Coppenhall High School

Britain

We are the British Britons
We go to work all day

We quite enjoy a Sunday roast
And driving to the coast

People come and people go
Britain's a trap, a rip-off too

The weather is so appalling
In Britain it's quite boring

We have tea
Not coffee

The transport isn't up to scratch
On trains and buses you have to catch

Ours is a land so small
People think we're really poor

God rule Britannia
Britannia rules the world.

Alex Vernon (12)
Coppenhall High School

England Team

There's one best thing about our team,
They've always got their national theme,
All the players take one shot,
As all the team goes so, so hot,
Beckham, Scholes, Owen and Butt,
If they don't score, the crowd goes tut,
Try one more time, they'll send shivers down your spine,
Speeding down the pitch,
Like playing the game called Quidditch.

Lee Doran (12)
Coppenhall High School

Lucy!

Lucy from the Fast Food Rockers,
Oh my god, she don't half shock us.
She is great and not at all shy,
But what she likes is scoffing pie.

I think she's fab, I think she's great,
She's probably dying for a long lasting break.
Lucy eats egg, sausage and chips,
She licks her fingers and smacks her lips.

Lucy likes chips and fish,
But when she piles on, she just makes a wish.
Crewe is where she grew up, so pretty,
She's got a sweet face like a baby kitty.

At their concerts people scream so loud,
Her parents watching, looking really proud.
Crewe is there and always aware,
We'll let her know that Crewe really cares.

She enjoys her food from the chippy,
But when she's finished, she's quite lippy.
Crewe is cold with loads of mould,
Lucy loves Britain, that's what I've been told.

Kirstie Taylor (13)
Coppenhall High School

The Life Of A Shop!

I open in the morning and I close at night,
When people pull my racks,
It gives me such a fright,
They shove and shout
And move all about,
It's such a pain,
Then it starts all again!
They come to the changing rooms,
Their hearts full of bliss,
They ask their friend, 'Is my bum big in this?'
I answer, 'Yes,' but they don't hear at all,
Good job really, they might break down the wall!
They come to the counter with all of their dosh,
Walking over, acting real posh,
She gives in her money, clutching her skirt,
Thinking at the party, she'll be a real flirt,
But I've seen it all, I know the truth,
Her bum looks so big,
Her flab hanging loose,
Nobody is good enough for my old shop,
The clothes are always absolute top,
When your mum sees the clothes, she'll have a fit,
So if you ever come, you better *watch it!*

Coral Fleet (12)
Coppenhall High School

English National Football Team

The manager leads out his men
And the manager's name is Sven
The big goalie is David James
The defenders always get the blame
The left-back player is Ashley Cole
If you foul him he'll use a fake roll
Tall centre-back is Ferdinand
Try tackle him, he's as tough as a shelf-stand
Beside Rio is Sol Campbell
Come near him, he'll make the ground rumble
Right back is Gary Neville
He's part of Man U, so he's a Red Devil
On the wing is Owen Hargreaves
He lives near the bushes with the green leaves
In the centre is Paul Scholes
Watch out, he can score amazing goals
Alongside him is Steven Gerrard
He's a scouser and thinks he's well hard
Right-wing is captain David Beckham
Watch his boots, you might wreck 'em
Up front on the left is Michael Owen
If he doesn't get his way he will start moaning
Then the youngster loony Wayne Rooney
Pulls a mooney in front of George Clooney.

Alex Williams (12)
Coppenhall High School

Five Little Puppy Dogs

Five little puppy dogs
Sitting by a door
One ran off
Then there were four

Four little puppy dogs
Went to play out on the tree
One fell off
Then there were three

Three little puppy dogs
Went out to Crewe
One got run over
Then there were two

Two little puppy dogs
Having lots of fun
One got lost
Then there was one

One little puppy dog
Sitting by the phone
He ran home
Then there were none.

Sammy Norris (13)
Coppenhall High School

Five Little Dinosaurs

Five little dinosaurs
Sharpening their claws
One saw a big T-rex
Then there were four

Four little dinosaurs
Scratching at a flea
One jumped into the lake
Then there were three

Three little dinosaurs
So cold they turned blue
One froze to death
Then there were two

Two little dinosaurs
Sniffing at a bomb
The bomb went off
Then there was one

One little dinosaur
All the rest had gone
He became extinct too
Then there were none.

Ashley Broomhall (13)
Coppenhall High School

Five Little Fishermen

Five little fisherman
One thought it was a bore
He fell in
Then there were four

Four little fishermen
Climbing up a tree
One fell off
Then there were three

Three little fishermen
Mending their rods with glue
One of them snapped
Then there were two

Two little fishermen
Trying to catch a swan
One got bit
Then there was one

One little fisherman
All his friends had gone
He packed away too
Then there were none.

Tom Birchall
Coppenhall High School

The Curse Of The Dreaded Soog

In the jungle of the rainforest,
there lies deep beneath the trees,
a mysterious creature known as Soog,
who lives on nothing but fish and bees.

Soog only comes out at night,
where the night is warm and still,
the creatures all hide away,
before Soog moves in for the kill.

One eye, one ear,
two arms on each side,
green all over,
wouldn't be looked at twice by a bride.

Soog hunts for his favourites,
sometimes he gets what he wants,
if he doesn't get his prize,
he will hunt for the prey some other way.

Lee Cartwright (13)
Coppenhall High School

The Lonely Aliens

In the big Milky Way,
Where the aliens fly then stay,
On the Martian ground,
There isn't too much sound.
But their big black eyes
And mouths like pies,
Are watching slowly,
As they feel oh so lonely.
They never come out,
There's goo all about!
So, the next time you go off to Mars,
In what they call a space car,
Remember that they are really shy,
So take the time to say, 'Goodbye!'

Hannah Straine-Francis (14)
Coppenhall High School

The Thing

Hey!
Let go!
What is this?
It has got green hair,
It is bigger than a bear!
It has two pairs of ears,
The thing grabs me and cheers,
It has got sharp teeth
And huge webbed feet.
I guess it is hungry
And on the menu is me!
It has got eight scaly toes
And a belly button that glows.
Fire comes from its nose!
What? Fangs? It has got hundreds of those,
It has got slippery green skin.
I can't tell whether it is fat or thin,
Bulging eyes and yellow veins -
Its fingers grip like freezing chains.
It is okay,
It has gone away,
It was a creature from space,
With a very hideous face!

Mathew Robinson (13)
Coppenhall High School

I Am An Alien!

I am an alien from outer space
My spaceship goes at a slow pace

I live on a planet called Spore
It would help if I could tell you more

I am two foot three
And I am up to your knee

I've got six legs
And my feet smell like eggs

There is only twenty of my kind
And there's one that's stuck on my mind

I live in a cold, dark cave
I am so hairy I need to shave

My name is Emo
See you soon, got to go!

Bernadette Cooke (13)
Coppenhall High School

Rabbits

Rabbits are furry and soft,
Big and small their sizes are.

Rabbits are different colours,
Grey, brown, white and black.

Rabbits eat different foods,
Mine likes carrots and apples best.

Rabbits like to hop around,
At night, mine likes to sleep,
Safe and sound.

Katherine Winstanley (12)
Coppenhall High School

Strange Visitor

I saw a thing that came from outer space,
There was two of them, they were having a race,
One was red, the other was green,
Their heads were the shape of a giant bean,
Their ears were sticking out larger than their heads,
The speed of their running was faster than mopeds,
They had no body, just three arms and legs,
They had bumps on their heads, they were the shape of eggs,
Their feet were like footy boots because they had grips,
Their toes were the shape of McDonald's chips,
Their noses were big, their eyes were square,
They were fluffy all over like a bear,
I was watching all this hiding behind a tree,
Then suddenly there was a noise from behind me,
I turned around and couldn't believe my eyes,
The UFO stories were a pack of lies,
Instead the shape was an immense ball,
It was big like Freeport shopping mall,
Then with no help, the things started floating high,
Into the spaceship, in towards the sky,
Then with a bright orange flame they blasted away,
From where they left off was a green and red ray.

Matthew Morris (13)
Coppenhall High School

Bonfire Night

Fireworks, fireworks, what do they do?
If you look at Guy Fawkes that will give you a clue.
When is Bonfire Night?
Erm . . . 5th November, I'm sure that's right.
I do like fireworks but the rockets are loud,
I look up at the sky and see what they are like
But all I see is a great big cloud.
Later on the sky starts darkenin',
So let's finish the night with a slice of parkin'.

Adam Shaw (11)
Hyde Technology School

Good In Evil, Evil In Good

It's strange how a soldier can do good by killing,
It's strange how a terrorist can love, care and think of
                                        actions as good,
There's always good in evil, but there's always evil in good.

I once heard of a man called Hitler, who decided to destroy the Jews,
They say he was as evil as the Devil for burning the Jews,
But no one can be pure evil can they?
No, not when he had a wife he cared, loved and looked after.

I once heard of a doctor called Shipman who decided to kill
                                        over a hundred patients,
They say he was as evil as the Devil for killing his patients,
But no one can be pure evil can they?
No, not when he helped and healed thousands of patients.

It's strange how a soldier can do good by killing,
It's strange how a terrorist can love, care and think of
                                        actions as good,
There's always good in evil, there's always evil in good.

Daniel Papworth (13)
Hyde Technology School

Snowy Day

The snow,
The soft white blanket on the ground,
Not moving or making any sound,
Building snowmen in the snow
And the laughter of the children,
Which will grow and grow.

The snow,
The soft white trodden snow,
The snow,
Falling from the sky like a broken star,
The snow.

Nicola Greenhalgh (11)
Hyde Technology School

It

It creeps as silent as the wings of an owl,
It scutters like a lizard in the darkness,
Its eyes glow like that of a wolf,
As it watches its prey closely.

To some it is as big as a blue whale,
Yet to others it is as tiny as a tick,
It climbs like a bear on a hill,
Waiting for the moment to strike.

Its back is as hairy as a dog's,
Its legs as skinny as a giraffe's neck,
It's as sleek as a puma,
Yet it is feared like a scorpion.

It jumps like a kangaroo
And strikes like a lion,
Yet now it strikes, it does not get the prey,
The prey gets it!

Joe Swindells (11)
Hyde Technology School

On My Own

Cruisin' on my scram
On the track,
My mates aren't here, they're on the tram,
But there's no turning back,
Razzed up a ramp, pulled a pancake whip,
Shot up another like a roller coaster and landed a backflip.

I tried my best
And my heart's pounding, I need to rest,
I'll sleep tonight and try again,
Who knows maybe tomorrow they'll get the train.

Sean Cookney (14)
Hyde Technology School

The Last Lion!

Look at the lion,
Come and see the last one,
The year is now 2021,
Look at the last lion,
It's lost its mum and dad,
It just lays there all alone,
Very, very sad.

Come and see the lion,
It's the only one,
It's here now with no family,
Their lives have been and gone,
It is so very special,
To come and see the last one,
Because of all those hunters,
Who have killed them one by one!

Simon Bradshaw (12)
Hyde Technology School

Change

When lightning strikes its way through the cloud,
It reminds me of his blade-like words,
Slitting, screaming through my soul aloud,
The sounds and sights make my blood curl.

Perfect pictures formed my mind
And the burden came along, 'twas you,
Now the pictures have long since died,
I'm no longer the person you once knew.

Jenny Barth (13)
Hyde Technology School

True Love

A beaming smile appears
Like a light on my face when you and I meet
And I can't help it when my heart begins to skip
And leap to a beat.

My head holds your image,
I keep seeing you around
And when I hear your voice
It's such a soothing beautiful sound.

Your voice is like the ocean, deep and wide,
Your whisper is the stream running by my side
And the way I feel for you, I hope you'll feel for me,
I hope it will last for all eternity.

When I'm lying beneath my quilt,
I block out all but you
And then I wonder
Could my love be true?

When I am so young
With all my life ahead of me,
Will I still love you,
My sweet friend, Rosie?

Scott Leigh (11)
Hyde Technology School

Friends

Friends are like one big family
They split but can be fixed
Friends are gold, any amount greater than life
Friends are solid, loyal, loved, stood by and helped
Friends are what you are to them
If not, you should talk it through
You love them, they should love you too.

Kimberly Bradwell (11)
Hyde Technology School

Fire

Like the angel of death it swiftly kills,
Lighting up forests and burning down hills,
Stealthily approaches, gives no warning,
Once it seizes you there's no running,
Once it confines you, you're in a cage,
However it dwindles, after its vicious rampage.

The gentle flame warms the cold,
The soft colours, red, orange, gold,
It will decorate the night sky,
The exploding colours revealing high,
It slowly flickers, lights up the dark,
As calm and soothing as the song of the lark.

It digests the blistered paint with flare,
With every encounter it expresses a glare,
As it devastates and engulfs its way,
It will devour all its prey,
Roaming, rampaging, uncaring,
Destroying, demolishing, exterminating.

Adam Leadbetter (13)
Hyde Technology School

Spring

I awake and look and wonder why,
The dark clouds have left the pretty blue sky.
Leaves start to appear on the once naked tree,
Oh I wonder what this could be?
I look to my garden from my once dark room
And see my flowers start to bloom.
Then all of a sudden the birds begin to sing
And then I realise it's the start of spring.

Danielle Davies (13)
Hyde Technology School

The Game

The crowd roared like a fighter jet revving up as twenty-two players
stepped onto the football pitch in flashy, colourful football kits.
The battle has begun!

There was a blast like a gunshot from the referee's whistle
as the ball started darting across and along the pitch.
Hearts heaving and eyes darting,
the crowd seethed as if watching gladiators in a ring.

The players moved as if an army, anticipating each other's moves
like an intricate dance motion.

The ball was fired at the net as powerful as a missile squeezing
its way to a target, the keeper flew across the net like a superhero
towards the direction of the shot, punching the ball out of the danger.

Four of the opposite team manoeuvre through the opposition in a
counter attack, gliding along the field in a line of skill and passion,
passing and turning. The forward man makes a run, speeding towards
the goal like a rocket. An enemy man jumps at him and knocks him
down in pain.
A yellow card is held in the air and a free kick on the edge of
the area is given.

The ball reaches the back of the net and my stomach flips
and flies in my mouth. The crowd omits an ear-splitting, splendid roar
as the final whistle is blown and the battle is won!

Disappointment hangs over the losers like an unwelcome ghost,
as the twenty-two men are cheered and saluted from the pitch.
The flags wave and the soldiers triumphant, embrace the crowd!

Jason Chetwyn (13)
Hyde Technology School

Good Is In Evil

In Hyde town centre
There is a building
A building where an
Evil man once worked
Good is in evil

Harold Shipman is the evil man
Evil in most ways
But nice in others
Death was his plan!

Killing people
Murdering them
For no reason at all!

Inserting lethal injections
Giving people drugs
Patients that were healthy
Such an evil man
Evil!

At home he could be nice
Loving to his family
His patients trusted him
Trusted
Good is in evil

Bin Laden, evil!
Killed thousands of innocent people
For no reason at all
Bin Laden blew up the Twin Towers
Murder!

All those poor people
Dead!
Because of him!

He was probably a loving person
Who loved his family
There are people who are sick!
But can be loving in other ways

There is good in evil
And it is all around us.

Katie Dodd (13)
Hyde Technology School

The Dangers Of Love!

Love is normally warm and bright,
But sometimes it could give you a fright.

You may love someone and need their heart,
But he doesn't love you back and it tears you apart.

First, you're not bothered and you'll just give a sigh,
But then you realise, a tear trickles by.

You tell someone close to get it out in the air
And tell them life is simply just not fair.

You sit through hours sobbing through pain,
Slowly and gradually going insane.

You watch your love stroll down the street
And feel your heart's drumming beat.

Suddenly you build up with rage,
Like an untamed beast locked in a cage.

You see he is not worth the heartache,
From all the weeping you need a break.

Finally, eventually, you move on,
You find someone loving, your soulmate,
The one.

Sophie Connaughton (13)
Hyde Technology School

Dr Shipman, An Evil Doctor

There was a man
Who killed his patients
Evil as a demon
Has a wife called Primrose
Who he loved and cared for
But when it came to his job
Then he became more serious
His patients didn't know what was heading their way
Killed mainly women, but what people want to know is
Why did Harold do it?
The pain his patients' relatives must have been going through
Must have been absolutely dreadful, heartbreaking

Dr Shipman must have killed at least 100 people
It's a good job that he is in prison
Could anyone be as evil as Dr Shipman?
Primrose didn't know that her husband was killing people
But when she did find out, she stood by him
She didn't believe that he did it
But we all know that he did
I wonder what was going through Dr Shipman's mind
When he was doing this awful thing to his patients
He was a mass murderer
Mrs Kathleen Grundy (one of his patients)
Had left her £200,000 home to Mr Shipman in her will
But it was a forged signature by Mr Shipman
Kathleen Grundy was a former mayor of Hyde
And was a regular member of the congregation.

Andrew Flanagan (13)
Hyde Technology School

There Was A Man . . .

In the dark, ghostly country of Germany,
Lived an evil man,
In that man was not blood,
In that man's head was not happy thoughts
But death
Wherever he walked
The thousands he killed would walk with him
The trees' leaves would suddenly drop
If they saw him approach towards them
His name was . . .

His name was known all over
Yet not known on the so-called Earth
He was the evilest person on the globe
He was
Hitler!

Zayd Islam (13)
Hyde Technology School

Love Poem

Love is a term that shouldn't be thrown around,
It is not to be given, it is to be found,
Between two people who are deeply in love,
It floats around like a chemical gas
And gives those two people a little shove,
Closer to each other until they kiss,
Now they begin to experience love and bliss,
It is now they decide they want to live together
And spend the rest of their lives together,
This is how love moves around,
Bringing people together, tightly bound.

Jake Iles (13)
Hyde Technology School

We're Off!

It was a dark, cold morning,
The players were up yawning.
The pitch was a rained on hill,
It was like it was an abandoned battlefield,
Waiting for the next war.

As the players start to warm up,
Running from side to side,
The crowd builds up from far and wide,
Now as the manager steps up to speak,
There is no sound, not even a peep.

The other team, all dressed in yellow,
Starting to train, they are not mellow.
Stepping up to take the kick,
Heads or tails, it's all in the flick.

Up it goes . . .
Tails!
We get to start the war,
Waiting for that dreaded shot,
To start the story and tie the knot,
It blows, *we're off!*

Marc Kurucz (13)
Hyde Technology School

The Chase!

She hurries through the gates as the school bell rings
Couldn't possibly bear to receive another punch
She saw them coming up behind her with smug looks on their faces
Started walking quickly, getting ready for the chase.

Laura Gooding (13)
Hyde Technology School

The Tiger's Normal Day

As the tiger makes his way through the boundless jungle,
Other animals become alarmed and afraid,
For his last victim has been left in a bundle,
Dead, lifeless, just another meal for the tiger made.

Under the shade of exotic canopy and trees,
The tiger takes what appears to be a rest,
A nearby prey takes its chance and flees,
This irritates the tiger, so he chases it his best.

Speed, strength and composure was how the tiger caught his prey,
Two bites was all it took to make the kill,
For testing the tiger, its life it would pay,
So small and weak, not even the tiger's stomach would it fill.

As darkness fills the clear sky,
The tiger finds a quiet place to stay,
He thinks nothing of the eventful past hours, you may wonder why,
Because to the tiger, this is a normal day.

Nathan Whittaker (13)
Hyde Technology School

Everyone Could Be Friends!

Friendship is like magic,
When you need a friend she's there,
Friendship is like superglue,
You have the strength to stick together,
But friendship can break up,
Although you'll always join again,
True friends bring each other happiness
And if all the world should catch a smile,
Everyone would be friends,
If there was no such thing as jealousy,
Everyone would be friends,
If the world would care for each other,
Everyone would be friends!

Natalie Griffiths (13)
Hyde Technology School

Death!

I could picture you sleeping beneath a mound of shrivelled leaves,
Then I would whisper you our moments below the blossomed trees,
When death decides to greet me, may we meet again,
Just to see that smile on your face, my dear trusted friend,
Tears began to water, as I thought of the days gone by,
When the life I have lived comes to an end,
I hope to die beneath a calm and crystal sky,
I would drown myself in my tears, yearning for you to come home,
As I sit and mourn in my bed silently on my own,
When death told me we were to meet again, it was music to my soul,
My body began to break and bleed and my life began to roll,
As we travel to God's kingdom only on a tide,
You must take death slowly, stride by stride,
I may be deprived of you and your love for me,
Please will you wait for me below the blossomed trees.

Robyn Leigh (13)
Hyde Technology School

Fairies!

A fairy is a friendly creature
A fairy is as clever as a teacher

Fairies are kind and soft
You might find fairies in your loft

A fairy is as light as a feather
Fairies sometimes hide in heather

Fairies can fly high above
Fairies are filled with love

Fairies are like beautiful pink roses
Fairies like to do poses

If you ever see a fairy
Don't be frightened, they are not scary.

Lauren McDermott (13)
Hyde Technology School

Love!

Love is special, it comes from the heart,
Sometimes it hurts when you're apart,
But if you're strong and don't let go,
Your love for each other will grow and grow.

Love is precious,
You cannot deny,
Sometimes it makes you laugh
And sometimes it makes you cry.

So hold on tight to the ones you love
And your life will be as easy as it is above,
So remember when you break up,
You should always try to make up.

Katie Croft (13)
Hyde Technology School

Wars!

We've got wars going on in the world we're living in
Children have no future or follow their destiny,
All around there's guns and swords,
Children born in a world that's torn,
Not just destroying the enemy but your friends,
Lots of deaths and injuries,
The world will soon be like a big grave,
We all need to communicate,
Put our hands up high, ask for a helping hand,
We can't just blow pixie dust and wave our wands,
Wars don't decide who's right, just who is left,
Young lives snatched away,
Like candy from a baby,
It's all rotten theft!

Ruksana Begum (13)
Hyde Technology School

You

Jumping hurdles every day
Just to dodge the words that are fired at you
You make up excuses
You hand in a forged note
Anything to stop them hurting you

Like 10 thousand bulls
Coming at you at the speed of light
You try to run
You try to hide
But soon they will find you

Like a frightened cat, you're scared of a dog
You are the tortoise racing against the hare
You go into an empty room
You lock the wooden door
And you cry yourself to sleep.

Fathema Johura (13)
Hyde Technology School

Love!

Love is like . . .
A metal chain of links
Which is never-ending,
Romance with the scent
Of red roses.
Love is like . . .
Diamonds glistening
Brightly in the sunlight,
A cinema full of hugs,
Kisses, hearts and presents.
Love is like . . .
A flower blossoming
More and more each day,
Future holidays with
Families and romance.

Natasha Lee (13)
Hyde Technology School

I Dream Of Peace

A harsh life of criminal brutality,
Not one I like to see,
It always ends where it begins,
Crime is surely one of their sins.

Nobody admits to growing insanity -
It's like a spreading fire growing hotter and hotter,
Deep inside they're all terrified of criminal brutality,
Hopefully you'll all hear my song,
That crime is wrong.

There are people killing, people dying,
On every street there are people crying,
As if they have nothing to live for,
Our homes are not a safe place to be anymore,
Do you think this is right? I don't.

Every day you will expect to hear,
The venerable sound of a police siren, incredibly near,
This is becoming a part of our everyday lives,
You know it shouldn't be.

People don't seem to know that the good have rights,
They think crime is acceptable,
They say they can't do anything to put crime right,
Maybe if they tried -
They will discover they can -
Crime is just like a fire that will never decrease
Unless you act upon it.

So this just totally needs to be said,
I'm sure you'll all admit,
We must fight this fire of crime and hate,
Stand up for ourselves and wipe out fate.

Furthermore when we have fought this foe,
You will definitely all come to believe,
We can overcome crime and fill our world with peace.

Amy Bredbury (13)
Hyde Technology School

Moon

A ghostly ship sailing across the ocean
Moving swiftly in one motion
Silver strands streak through the sky
So delicate, impossible to define
Reflections cast upon the waves
Appears to be drowning, only to be saved
Ripples shimmering
Water glimmering
It's magical
A mystery
With prehistoric history
Passing through treacherous surroundings
A never-ending voyage
Encircling the Earth's boundaries
A disappearing act that's hard to follow
Goodnight moon,
I'll see you tomorrow.

Erin Bourke (12)
Loreto Grammar School

Lonely

Lonely is a boy lost on the moor,
Lonely is a poor man knocking at the door.
Lonely is waiting, looking for a sign,
Lonely is mourning for families over time.

Lonely is the ruler in his hall of stone,
Lonely is friendless playing on his own.
Lonely is a puppy waiting at the door,
Then the owner comes home, lonely no more.

Lizzy Carr (11)
Loreto Grammar School

The Crying Game

Imagine being all alone,
Nothing but skin and bone.
You hear the gunshot which seems so distant,
Then hear the horrific screams in an instant.

You long for merciful love,
As you believe in the heavens above.
But still you wait your turn in line to die
And when the time strikes, you ask 'Why?'

Don't cry my child,
Keep your faith up all the while,
I know how you feel too,
For I once was just like you.

So don't cry my child,
I feel your pain.
For I know how you play,
The crying game . . .

Olivia Doody (11)
Loreto Grammar School

Firework Night

Glistening, glittering, blazing bright,
Fireworks sparkle through the night.
Shooting through the starry sky,
Cascades of colours begin to fly.

Spurts of orange, spurts of red,
All the cats and dogs have fled.
Rockets dart up ever so loud,
Splitting up the night-time cloud.

But be careful, they can hurt,
When the flames of the bonfire spurt.
They can burn or even kill,
Just stand back and enjoy the thrill!

Briony Johnstone (11)
Loreto Grammar School

Mum Thinks This And That . . .

Mum thinks I'm a girly girl,
But I'm really not that kind,
I'm a sort of tomboy
And her fashion's way behind!

Mum thinks I like porridge,
But I'm really not that kind,
I'm a sort of junk food person
And her cook book's way behind!

Mum thinks I should be a tidy person,
But I'm really not that kind,
I'm a sort of an untidy slob
And her duster is way behind!

Catherine Chapman (11)
Loreto Grammar School

What Would I Like To Be?

I'd like to be a doctor and cure the sick,
I'd like to be an athlete but I ain't that quick.
I'd like to be an actress and get paid quite a lot,
But I'd definitely love to be a teacher . . . *ha . . . not!*
I'd like to be a comedian but I'm not that funny,
Whatever it is I'd have to be paid a lot of money.
There must be something out there for me,
What would I like to be?

Anna Kaczmarczyk (11)
Loreto Grammar School

My Teacher

Dear Lord up in Heaven,
Please her me, I'm only 11.
My teacher has lovely hair,
But not at all like a bear.
She's into sport,
She always has the ball caught.
She quickly puts it in the net,
To be honest, I'm glad we met.
Dear Lord hear my prayer,
I don't want her to turn out like a pear.
Look after her well,
'At last!' she says, 'I'm saved by the bell!'
She never ever falls on her knees,
Neither does she get stung by swarming bees.
Her chest isn't hairy,
Not like a gorilla.
She loves ice cream,
Her favourite's vanilla, she absolutely loves football,
She likes it more than me,
She even knows more about it than the man on TV.

Katie Edwards (11)
Loreto Grammar School

Poetry

P aul wanted some money,
O f course he had to ask his mummy,
E ddie had twenty-five pounds,
T o get to his house he had to cross the school grounds.
R odney, his dog, had to go with him,
Y et in the end there was no need
because Eddie was out spending it!

Heather Nicholson (11)
Loreto Grammar School

The Sea!

The blue waves came into shore
As I began to tour,
The crystal coral reef,
The warm water beckoned me,
I couldn't wait to see,
What lay beneath.

The waves crashed onto the sand,
The sea came into land
And pulled against my feet,
As I floated on the salty waves,
Crabs burrowed into the sandy cave,
To escape the blazing heat.

The singing dolphins danced
And pranced,
The sun began to rise,
As I swam into the sea,
It felt to me,
That there could be no greater prize.

Emma Becque (11)
Loreto Grammar School

My Everlasting Love

Dear ?
I love you from the bottom of my heart
That's the reason why I hope we never part
I'll love you forever
My most precious treasure
I'll always keep you close and never let you go
We'll stay together for all time
And so forever treasure this rhyme.

Naomi Aisueni-Page (13)
Loreto Grammar School

Changing Weather

The sun does shine most every day
In the most gleaming way
It hangs above the world you see
And sits there very happily
It's like a bulb
One thousand watts
That every day rocks and rocks
From side to side
To share the light
Give day to all the world

The frost does come
(So does the sun)
And as we're told
Jack has come to stay
He doesn't come for very long
And then he goes away

The rain does drop
Never seems to stop
It always leaves you wet
And not once yet
Has someone not complained
About the dripping dropping pouring loads of rain

The weather changes day to day
Each one comes then goes on its way
The weather changes day to day
The sky is blue, black or grey
The weather changes day to day
I love the sun
Hip hip hooray!

Alex Hulme (11)
Loreto Grammar School

Zack

He's shaggy and hairy,
Loveable too.
He's cuddly and small,
But I think he's grew.

I love to ride him everywhere,
Especially cantering,
To trot is like a dream on him,
It feels like he's got wings.

His nose is soft like velvet,
His mane is silky and slick,
His eyes bright and alert,
I like to brush him all the time,
To keep him clean is the trick.

I love him with all my heart,
Until this love would bend,
He is so playful
And will always be my special friend.

I suppose you're wondering who he is,
The animal I'm writing about?
He is my pony
And he will never be lonely,
Because I love him so . . .

Olivia Brett (11)
Loreto Grammar School

Football

Twenty-two men kicking a ball,
It's such a ridiculous game,
But then again I am a girl,
So who wouldn't think the same?

When I watch our colour screen telly,
All I see is bony bellies,
Showing themselves on display -

To a loud crowd
Who are clapping
And cheering
And shouting
And booing

And I know it's weird,
But I sit there too
And I keep on wooing!

Sydney Keough (11)
Loreto Grammar School

Splodge, My Cat

Splodge, my cat, is black and spotty
His fur is all around the house
My mum says that he drives her potty
Last night I saw him chase a mouse

Splodge, my cat, is incredibly lazy
All he does is eat and sleep
At times my dad is driven crazy
Then shouts at him and make *me* weep

But Splodge, my cat, we all adore
By the fire he lies all curled
Goodness me, he won't lift a paw
But we wouldn't trade him for the world!

Ellen Shaw (11)
Loreto Grammar School

The Mysterious Dream

I can't believe that dream was true,
You were included in it too.
We were flying through the sky on clouds
And looking down at all the crowds.

We met some birds called Jill and Jane,
They were twins but didn't look the same.
We met two swans called Matt and Phil,
Even though they had feathers, they still caught a chill.

We met two planes called Chad and Jack,
One was red and one was black
And we met two pigs called Bill and Bob,
They said they'd escaped from death on the hob.

In the end, I slowly woke up
And picked up my reading book,
Inside it had a story of a girl,
Who had very long fair hair but had a curl.

She went for a ride upon a cloud
And looked down at crowds and crowds.
She dreamt she saw a bird and swan
And said she'd seen another one.

She thought she saw some pigs and planes,
But said her mind was playing games.
Soon she got up and looked around
And laughed as her fair curls hit the ground . . .

Rachael Roberts (11)
Loreto Grammar School

Can I Have A Pony?

'Mum, can I have a pony?
I'll be ever so good,
It won't roll around in the mud,
We will get it in May or in a day,
I'll even buy its hay
And maybe call it Bay.'
'Just go and pester your father,' that's all she would say.

'Dad, please don't be mad,
But can I have a pony?
I promise it won't be bad.'
My dad just sighed when he looked into my eyes,
I slowly crept away and didn't see him
Until the end of the day.

I heard my mum and dad talk away
About getting me a pony for my birthday,
I just hoped they would say yes,
Maybe I could call it Tess,
Or Hope and Glory, that would be my best story.

Freddie Luscombe (11)
Loreto Grammar School

A Real Friend

What do you look for in a real friend, truth or lies?
What do you look for in a real friend, loyalty or dizziness?
What do you look for in a real friend, someone new and
unpredictable or you?
What do you look for in a real friend, action or dullness?
What do you look for in a real friend, calmness or franticness?
What do you look for in a real friend, happiness or grimness?
What do you look for in a real friend, joy or moodiness?
What do you look for in a real friend, peace or war?
What do you look for in a real friend, smiles or frowns?
What do you look for in a real friend, love or hate?
What do you look for in a real friend?
I look for you.

Róisín Shryane (12)
Loreto Grammar School

I Am A Cat

I am a cat,
Prowling at night,
Watching my prey,
Ready to fight.

I am a cat,
Sleeping on my pouffe,
Dreaming about,
What happens today.

I am a cat,
That loves to eat,
Fish and chicken
And different meat.

I am a cat,
That people love,
Marking my territory,
Catching a dove.

Now I am a cat,
Catching a pheasant,
I like the humans,
I'll give them a present.

Samantha Yates (11)
Loreto Grammar School

Fat

It clings to your thighs
It clings to your hips
Every time that chocolate touches your lips
You can try to hide it by dressing in colour or in black
But the will to diet is the thing I lack.

Helen Kilburn (12)
Loreto Grammar School

The Traffic Centre

All bags rustling
All people bustling
All girls chat
All pensioners sat
All babies crying
All mums sighing
At the traffic centre

All popcorn popping
All people shopping
All chips frying
All kids buying
All staff hired
All people tired
All coffee whirring
At the traffic centre

All palm trees green
All red coats seen
All yellow, blue and red
All shop sign colours I have said
All flashing sign lights
All at people's head heights
At the traffic centre

So this hustly, bustly place
Is all at a great pace
You all come here to shop
Once you get here, you can't stop
The sky is blue and so are you
Once you've done your shopping
I hope you will come back again
For another hour's bopping
At the Trafford Centre!

Emily Webster (11)
Loreto Grammar School

No Shoes!

I don't know what to do,
With that dog of mine,
He's run off with my school shoe
And covered it in slime!

I'll get into trouble,
With the teachers at school,
If I have lots of bubbles,
On my shoe (so uncool).

I could wear my trainers,
If I got past my mum,
But I can't find those, oh,
They were borrowed by my chum.

I don't know what to do,
I think I'll go back to bed,
Unless, I just wore,
My slippers instead!

Danielle Kane (11)
Loreto Grammar School

Love Poem

You are the one that comforts me and I do the same to you,
The one that knows when something is wrong,
The one that knows your favourite song,
The one I put no one else above,
The one I love,
I just can't control myself,
Can't be with no one else,
I need to find out who you are,
You may even be a star,
I'll search this world high and low,
So there'll be no sorrow
And when I find you, I'm sure I will,
We'll be together through thick and thin.

Thalia Farrell (13)
Loreto Grammar School

My Love Poem!

I have seen you at the bus stop,
I have seen you on the train,
I have seen you at the local shop
And even in the rain.

I love you like the sun loves the summer,
Like snow loves the winter,
Like golden leaves love autumn,
Like gambolling lambs love spring.

No one knows I love you,
No one knows I care,
My heart always skips a beat,
Every time you're there!

Enya Magill (13)
Loreto Grammar School

I've Seen You

I've seen you walking down the street,
You never seem to notice me.
I wait for you to come passing by,
But still you do not see.

I've seen you at the bus stop,
But I don't think you've seen me.
I get there early to wait for you,
It's like you cannot see.

When you're walking down the street,
I would like you to see.
When you're at the bus stop,
Please do notice me.

Rachel McPeake (13)
Loreto Grammar School

In My Heart

To my darling,
You light up the sky like a starling.
I love you more than words can say,
I never want you to go away.

I will always love you,
Even though you haven't a clue.
You make me go weak at the knees,
Like the buzzing of the bees.

You are always in my mind,
In my heart you will find:
My love for you,
I hope you love me too.

Let's not be apart,
For that will break my heart.
Your love helps me through the days,
My love always
?

Lucy Baxter (12)
Loreto Grammar School

An Ode To Love

Dearest?
To me you are a muse,
A place from which I draw inspiration,
With every twist and turn you make,
I come aglow with love,
Your habits may change, but my feelings do not.
Most vivid are my dreams I get from thinking of your smile,
I'd like to possess but one dark curl from your head.
I love you more than ever before,
To see you once more would make my life complete.

Morgan Tunney (12)
Loreto Grammar School

To My Dearest Darling True Love

I miss you so
But I have to know
Do you love me more than I know?
If you do
I will love you too
Then I will bring cuddles to you
I wish we were together by the Mediterranean Sea
So all our children can play happily
I wish my father would allow
To let us marry right now
I want to be married happily
On a tropical island by the sea
That is all I have to say
Until the day God takes me away
Lots of love
Your true love.

Claire Finnerty (12)
Loreto Grammar School

My Love

My love, that's what you are,
I love you so much, I can't bear to part,
When I see you in the street,
My heart skips a beat,
I adore your smile,
It's anything but vile,
Your lovely great hair,
The girls all love to stare.
I see you at night,
It's like I'm in darkness
And you're my shining light.

Claire McAdam (12)
Loreto Grammar School

Music

Music here
Music there
Music around me everywhere
From orchestras
To steel bands
Oh it makes me clap my hands!

At Christmas time
Sleigh bells ring
And carols we adore to sing
With prayers and hope
Then comes New Year
To celebrate with song and cheer!

Thirty-five years
Top of the Pops
With music hits and music flops
Rap and garage
Rock 'n' roll
Feel the rhythm in your soul!

Let's sing and dance
And have some fun
Music's good for everyone
It's number one
In every way
Please music, never fade away!

Amanda Mason (11)
Loreto Grammar School

A Love Poem For . . .

At one-thirty every Thursday,
I wait for you to come.
I watch the big hand strike six
And the little hand strike one.

You walk into my house,
My whole body goes numb.
Your hair waves in the wind,
Your eyes twinkle like the sun.

You walk into the front room
And sit down in your chair.
I watch you get your books out
And brush your golden hair.

I want to say I love you,
I want to say I care.
I run out of the room,
As I turn back to stare.

I can never say I love you,
Now that part is true.
It does not matter to me though,
I will love you forever true.

Ella McHugh (12)
Loreto Grammar School

Friendship

Friendship is something that's there for you and me,
Friendship is inviting a couple of friends over for tea.
Friendship is helping people when they're down,
Friendship is making them feel like they wear the crown.
Friendship is being nice and kind,
Friendship is helping people make up their mind.
Friendship is something that's made by two
And I hope that friendship is between me and you.

Natasha Gee (11)
Loreto Grammar School

A Love Poem

My darling dearest Christopher,
With your skin as soft as silk
And sometimes you wear those cute little specs,
On your eyes as white as milk.

I always want to help you,
You really are that useless.
But I know that deep inside your heart,
You're lovely and I must confess . . .

You're kind and sweet, quite funny too,
When you're near, my heart's a-flutter.
So next time when I meet with you,
Don't think that I'm a nutter.

Just know that I am deeply in love,
From the bottom of the Earth to the heavens above . . .

Katie Marshall (12)
Loreto Grammar School

True Love

T o you I give my love so great,
R eally, really, you are a great mate,
U sing your charm you are a real hit,
E verybody thinks you're fit.

L ong days are such a pain,
O nly until I see you again,
V ery complimentary you are to me,
E ven though we're only friends, that's all we'll ever be!

Louise Harrison (12)
Loreto Grammar School

The Way I Feel

I lie awake at night,
Thinking of you;
The way your voice sounds,
The way you smell,
The way you care for me,
Pretending to others
That we're just friends.

The times we've spent together,
In the park or just walking along,
There's something about you
'Cause every time you talk to me,
All words lose sense or meaning.

Me and you together,
For forever and a day.
Please tell me you love me too,
'Cause the way I feel,
Is so true, but if we stay the way we are,
My heart will break in two.

Natalie Rogers (12)
Loreto Grammar School

My Love Poem

B est friends that's what we are,
E verybody thinks you're a real star,
S miling is something you always do,
T hroughout the day I think of you.

F orever friends we will be,
R emember you're very close to me,
 I can always tell when you're sad,
E verybody normally feels really bad,
N ever have I told you how I really feel,
D reams and hopes I will never reveal.

Olivia Cashmore (12)
Loreto Grammar School

Best Friend

My best friend and me always row,
We're never not on each other's backs.
At break we never play together,
But keep our backs turned away,
In gym class we're never partners
And have never wanted to be.
Mrs Kelly always complains,
About us calling each other names.

Most of the time we're not on speaking terms
And never give Christmas presents,
I can't remember when we last looked each other in the eye,
Maybe it was a few years ago?
We always give each other cheek
And never say nice things,
We've never properly liked each other,
But of course I don't know why.

The day that we first met,
We were obviously a little shy
And that's when it all started,
The first time she made me cry,
We've known each other from nursery
And we've always been best pals,
That's the way it always will be,
Me and my best friend.

Bethany Harper (11)
Loreto Grammar School

Fireworks

Showering, cascading, hovering bright,
Sparkling and glittering over the dark night.
Striking colours all over the sky,
Blue, green, yellow and red flying high.

Birds flap, owls hoot, dogs howl and cats yelp,
Whimpering and weeping loudly for help.
Jumping with a sudden cry of fright,
Pets timidly lying in the corner with no light.

Sitting crying in the corner a boy,
Inside him not a little bit of joy.
With a sudden piercing scream that fills the night,
Too late, his mother shouts with fright!

Sinead Mitchell (11)
Loreto Grammar School

Flowers

Sunflowers and daisies all around they bloom,
A bunch of fresh lilies to scent my room.
A pattern of ivy weaves around my front door,
Buttercups, dandelions and many more.
The poplar trees sway when the wind gives a breeze,
The colourful holly bush stands out from the trees.
To the end of summer, leaves begin to fall,
All except the fir tree, which stays proud and tall.
The flower colours can be dull or bright,
Carnations and roses are a beautiful sight.

Kelly Smith (11)
Loreto Grammar School

Parents

Parents do this, children do that,
All parents do is chit chat,
Parents are there to give us hope
And help us with homework, so that we can cope,
But of course, that's not the case,
They just yell, 'Tie up your shoelace!'
If you help but do something wrong,
Trust me, you won't be outstanding for very long,
They blame it on you, no,
No matter what or who,
It's always you.

I hope you can see my warning,
I now try not to go into mourning,
I hope it is here,
Loud and clear,
Please take my advice and . . .
Run!

Tara Hook (11)
Loreto Grammar School

Ambling Through The Town

Ambling through the town
Pacing up and down
Watching carefully at my feet
As they plod along the street

Ambling through the town
Pacing up and down
Looking at my feet
Under my nose

Ambling through the town
Pacing up and down
Poking out the end
Are my ten little toes!

Natalie Mason-Salt (11)
Loreto Grammar School

Brussel Sprouts

Mum said
'Eat your Brussel sprouts'
But I'm not sure I can
I've not liked the look of them
Since they were in the pan

Give me chips or chocolate
I'll eat them with no fuss
Or creamy chicken korma
Accompanied by cous cous

But please don't give me Brussel sprouts
So round and hard and green
I hate the taste, I hate the smell
I wish I'd never seen
That ugly wrinkly vegetable
I really am not keen!

Laura O'Dea (11)
Loreto Grammar School

This Poet Is . . .

This poet is . . .
as cool as a cucumber,
as busy as a bee,
as delicate as a butterfly,
as calm as the sea.

This poet is . . .
as cheeky as a monkey,
as fast as a car,
as lovely as a white rose,
as bright as a star.

Lauren Braithwaite (11)
Loreto Grammar School

A Poem

'I'm going to write a poem'
I said to my mum
'That should be good fun!'

The pen and paper soon were found
The words in my head just spun around
A poem about what? I don't know a lot

A list of rhyming words
That's where I can start
About colours and friends and home and
Calm down, plan, use a chart

I tried and tried and tried in vain
To methodically produce a rhyme
But no, I haven't got the type of brain that produces verses
That capture the interest of the poetic at this present time

I thought of school and the good we do
When we smile at each other, meaning, 'Hello, how are you?'

The prayers at Mass
The songs we sing
The work in class
Oh! Every little thing

From getting up to greet the day
Sharing out thoughts and deeds in our special ways

I now realise my life is a poem
Ever changing, full of variety
No wonder I can't get going with my poem
There's so much to say I can't manage it in one day.

Khryscilla Rowbotham (11)
Loreto Grammar School

Love

Love is such a funny thing
You fall in and you fall out
But if the love you feel is true
Surely there should be no doubt?

Loving you brings a smile to my face
It sweeps me off my feet
The blink of your eyes and the look of your smile
Makes my heart miss a beat

I know you're here right next to me
Yet you haven't said a word
The warmth is felt within our hearts
And silent love is heard.

Aimée Harragan (13)
Loreto Grammar School

Love Poem

My dearly beloved,
Words cannot describe the way I feel for you inside,
Your dark brown hair and twinkling blue eyes fill me with delight,
It would be my wildest dream if I could be your bride,
The moment I saw you, I knew you were just right,
My love for you is unbreakable,
I hope you see this is true,
My love for you is unmistakeable,
Because darling, I love you!

Sarah Henry (13)
Loreto Grammar School

Come Unto Me

Come unto me,
Be lured unknowingly,
To your death in the deep, to your very last sleep.
See me jump, see me dive,
As you'll wriggle and writhe,
When you die in the deep, fall into your very last sleep.
I shall flick, you will foam,
Become part of my home,
Come die into the deep and sleep your last sleep.

A thrashing snake,
Babbles and bubbles,
Fall unto it, it shall swallow your troubles.
Slipping and sliding,
Down you shall go,
Your sleep won't be painful, but tranquil and slow.
You shall sway side to side,
Jump and fall with the tide,
Feel the damp, hear the hiss, swallowed up by sleep's bliss.

Your crying shall mingle,
With the sea's gentle tingle,
That is sloshing you up, like the soup that you've supped.
For if I cannot leave,
Then I shall bring in
All those who venture far out, be them hers or a him.

So beware little ones,
Beware of my tides
And always remember, don't get on my wrong side.
Stay well away,
Don't venture too far,
Or your spirit shall fly and become a star!

Anna Perry (12)
Ryles Park High School

Poetry In Motion

Who's lazy?
I'm not lazy,
I'm not tired,
I don't have bags under my eyes,
I'm not yawning,
I'm not falling asleep,
But I do hate getting up in the morning!

It's strange,
My eyes hurt,
My legs are shaking,
I need sleep,
But I'm stuck *here*,
Trying to write a poem!

I nearly nodded off in German,
(No, it's true),
But the funny thing is,
I'm falling asleep
Right now,
Let me just rest my eyes,
Just for two seconds?
Please, Miss,

Pleazzzzzzzz.

William Nelson (14)
Ryles Park High School

Movement Of Dance

A simple song,
A simple dance,
It feels as if you are in a trance.

You don't care what people say,
You like to move in a different way.

A simple song,
A simple dance,
It feels as if you are in a trance.

You can feel the loud beat,
Then you start to move your feet.

A simple song,
A simple dance,
It feels as if you are in a trance . . .

Leann Huxley (14)
Ryles Park High School

The Devil And Hell

In my world it's as hard as Hell,
You almost feel like you've fell,
The flames are hot, the Devil's here,
I know it's time for me to fear,
I tremble terribly, I need some help,

There's no one there,
I'm lost in Hell . . .

Kirsty McCormack (14)
Ryles Park High School

Transport

I am gonna go so far
While I'm driving in my car
I hope I stay afloat
While I'm sailing in my boat
I was in a little train
When it just began to rain
I was thinking in my brain
When I saw a massive plane
It is time I must be going
It is time to end my poem

I am at a big bend

It's the end!

Kyle Fenton (14)
Ryles Park High School

Poetry In Motion

Underneath the starry sky,
I think of you and sometimes cry,
If I had a chance to see you again,
I'd never let you go back to them.
When I lie underneath the sky,
I make up pictures in my mind's eye,
They look like
The stars and the sky.

Leanne Brown (15)
Ryles Park High School

Fishing For Carp

A lot of people like to fish,
It's the best sport around.
The maggots, the tackle, the fish you catch,
You have to gobble them up.

A lot of them are colourful
And most of them look nice.
Of course there's some that don't,
I could make a list but I won't
As it would only drag on if I did.

Carp are quite slippy and slimy,
But can be shiny like a mirror underneath.
But boy, they must be thick to bite on a hook,
The first chance they get they take it and bite.

It's awful for them but perfect for us,
It's your tea nearly ready.
It took nothing to catch,
But fit for a king.

Ashley Bailey (12)
Ryles Park High School

Wrestling Tournament

W atching at the ringside
R eferee rings the bell
E veryone is silent
S lamming his opponent
T he tournament is underway
L ying flat on the mat
I njured and in pain
N othing happening
G oing nowhere.

Matthew Bennett (13)
Ryles Park High School

Fishing For Carp

I set my tackle up once again,
Hoping for a ghost carp,
I'm well prepared with bread and maggots
And vanilla sweetcorn galore.

I have a bite!
It's a tench which struggles
And snaps my line.
I cast out with floating bread,
A big ghost carp comes into sight.

He grabs the bread and with it the hook,
At last - I have a carp,
I pulled him in, he's over fifteen pounds,
What a catch,
This surely is the catch of the day.

Chris Heapy (13)
Ryles Park High School

Make Me Happy, Make Me Sad

When you're here and I am there,
There's nothing left for us to share.
Make me happy, make me sad.
I will love you through *good and bad.*
I will love you through *thick and thin.*
Maybe this is where we begin.
Take me to Heaven, take me to Hell,
Can't settle for anything in-between.

Lindsay Bailey (14)
Ryles Park High School

Me And You

Me and you, is it true?
'Cause what we had, makes me laugh
When I think about the time we had
I try not to make myself sad
'Cause lately I feel we've been growing apart
We're backwards instead of forwards
From finish to start
Was it meant to be you and me
United as one unity?

I feel lately we've been caught up in yesterday
Not thinking about today, or for what's coming tomorrow
All these emotions build up and I can't be happy
Because I am deeply saddened by sorrow
But one thing is for sure and I do know this
I will always cherish your first kiss
Or should I even be feeling this?
Should these feelings be here?
All I know about love is from TV
And what I hear by ear
My head is full of confusion, I don't know what to do
How am I supposed to say 'I love you'
No matter how much I try to fight it
I just can't hide it
I am in love with you, that's just the way it goes
I guess this is just another case of
The incurable disease.

Sammi Heywood (14)
Ryles Park High School

Fishing

I like going fishing
It's a relaxing day
I throw my bait in so the fish sniff it out
Then they take your bait
I rest my rod on my chair and on the rod rest
I will catch a carp
Then the hook goes through its lip
I fish at Mayfield Pond and at the River Bollin
You can catch trout
And at Mayfield Pond I catch roach
When I fish with maggots
The little sticklebacks come
And take the maggots
When you get the hook out of its mouth
It sticks its spikes
In your hands
When I am fishing, I eat all my food
I sit on my chair and eat all my chocolate biscuits
I love relaxing and resting
When I sit on my chair
Having a drink of orange juice
Catching fish.

Noel Boon (13)
Ryles Park High School

Bulldog

A bulldog runs at you and takes a biscuit
gently in its mouth.
A bulldog's muscular jaw chews it down
and gulps it down.

Thomas Bennett (12)
Ryles Park High School

Night And Day

When we wake up in the morning
The sun is shining at dawn
We get out of bed
And wake up our sleepy heads
We move our head from side to side
Get out on a very good side
Go downstairs and turn on the TV
Guess who we see on screen?
It's Avril Lavigne

We go to school
To brighten up the day
The teacher's rules
They feel the same way
In lunch we eat
Afterwards our mates meet

End of the school day
Hurrah, hurrah, hurrah
Have tea
Don't see
We go to bed
Mum has turned out the light
Now there's nothing in sight.

Chantelle Pelka (13)
Ryles Park High School

Olly

I have a friend
Who looks like a fish
His name is Olly
But we call him Wally
He's got a big mouth
It makes him look like a trout
He's cute and funny
But it's a shame he looks like a fish!

Stephanie Morrey (15)
Ryles Park High School

War

Every time I hear about war
I think to myself how silly;
To think people can kill
Other people -
Who may be someone else's relatives.

If I could stop the war, I would.
I would stand in the middle and say;
Could you please stop this?
Hating each other!
Because
In a way
You are hurting yourself.

Sarah Huxley (15)
Ryles Park High School

My Fastest Car

I have a super fast car in my garage
Which can go from 0 to 90 in under three seconds
I take it for racing competitions
And I never lose for my awesome speed
I move so fast my friends can't see me
Just because it's fast, doesn't mean it's good
It's the best car
Driven by me!

Luke Edwards (15)
Ryles Park High School

True Love

How can we explain love?
When I say the word, you may think of one idea
It could just be love for all
Or love for none
But if a person doesn't have love
What's wrong?
A person may love to hate
And hate to love
So still somewhere they have love
Love is a confusing word
Wouldn't you think?
Someone could have too much love
And greed on it until it shrinks
To have love is something special
To be able to give is better
Maybe you just want somebody to hold
Or for somebody to say that they would . . .
How can we explain love?

Claire Phillips (16)
Ryles Park High School

Granny's Lost Treasure

A bit of string,
An old gas bill,
A postcard from our Jenny,
Further down, a worming pill,
And a green and fluffy penny.
Down the back and through the crack,
I knew that I struck gold,
'I've found them Gran, down your chair,
False teeth, all green with mould!'

Laura McKeith (15)
Ryles Park High School

If I

If I ever had a chance to change my life
I would
I would turn back time if I could
If I could tell through right and wrong
I would say I will try to go the right way
I wish I could confess
Why my life is such a mess
But I couldn't
I shouldn't
I wouldn't
When I turn around and you're not here
I can feel a lonely tear
If only you could say
How happy you want me to be
And that I could be you
And you be me
Now you know how I feel
And when you're there
I know you really care.

Jody Harrison (13)
Ryles Park High School

Life

Life is good
Life is great
Life can be fun but also a shame
Life is like a merry-go-round
Round and round you go
Life is like a dream
You never want it to stop
Life carries on round and round
Till you get to the end
And it dies like us
Don't forget you live once
Enjoy life to the fullest.

Samantha Barton (15)
Ryles Park High School

Confrontation With Light

Each evening, I set alight my moment
The time where reality corresponds with utter mythology
The array of gilded absence
From the Mother Earth I am living with
Initiates the mind and magic
Of such confrontation
My small yet worthy country cottage
Disappears into the starlit eclipse
And I only see only the small bridge
Which connects one side of the bank to the other.
My less sophisticated fitness of my pro-dramatic walking
Staggers with the feeling of confrontation
Between stepping stones
And the tips of my toes
And I stop to the tune of the stream
Which is only obliged
To transport the god's own fish
And dead flower buds.
'Here are thy fairies' wings!'
A flying feather whispers in my ear
I turn and watch the scenery
While examining the time on my pocket watch
Two minutes past twelve and it is early
The fairies have already began to emerge
From the moon-corrupt stream
For them their magic is never too early.

Lee Fitzgerald (15)
Ryles Park High School

Contrasts

Under the sea there is life
Under the sea there is light

Under the sea there is death
Under the sea there is darkness.

Kimberley Lucas (16)
Ryles Park High School

Ferrari

F is for fast! 0-60 in 4.5 seconds and a top speed of 190mph.
E is for the engineering involved in making this 3900cc
    V8 12 cylinder engine,
R is for racing on a duel carriageway side by side with a
    Lamborghini at speeds of over 130mph,
R is for racing as fast as a bullet.
A is for the aerodynamics that keeps this car stuck on the road
    and lowered so you can hit corners at over 60mph,
R is for the rush you get when you win the race,
I n the end when you have won the race your Ferrari is safe
    away for another day.

Danny Hague (15)
Ryles Park High School

Friends = Buddies!

Friends are like having a family around you
Friends are there when you need support
Friends are there for you when you are stuck in a problem
Friends are there for you when you are lonely and bored
Friends are like your bodyguards!
Friends are there for laughs, giggles and fun, fun!
Friends are fun to go out with, especially going shopping with!
Friends are your best, best buddies for life on end!

Kirsty Forster (15)
Ryles Park High School

That's Love And A Maggot's Story
From Addicted To Love

When I was a kid
My father had a dog
It started to get weak and sickly
So he took it to the vet

The doctor thinks a maggot
Must have laid eggs in the dog's butt
Oh! Maggots, yuck!

Now the eggs have hatched
And now they have started to grow
And eventually some of them are going to eat the dog alive

When I said the maggots eating the dog alive
It might look like the dog getting eaten by maggot piranhas (giggles)
Ha ha ha ha ha (ahem) . . . sorry

Well anyway the doctor says it should be put to sleep
Because it's old anyway

But my father won't do it
He takes it home
He puts it on the bed
Then he starts to reach up into the dog
Picking up the maggots one by one
It takes him all night but
He gets every last one
That dog outlived my father
You know what it's called
That's love.

Sarah Brown
Ryles Park High School

Rush

I'm in a great rush
I'm late!
I jump in my fast car
And race to work
The traffic lights go red
I'm late!
I'm getting irritated
I keep tapping, go green, go green
Finally it turns to yellow to green
I'm getting later!
I'm nearly there, damn it!
There's no parking plots
I've very late
I'm waiting again
I am gritting my teeth
Thank God there's a parking plot
I run as fast as I can to my boss
'I'm very sorry
That I am late'
'It's OK.'

Jamie Cleaver (12)
Ryles Park High School

Liverpool Are Great

G reat Liverpool
E very time I watch, they win
R ight in the net there is always a ball
R eally they are the best team going
A sk my dad if you think I am wrong
R isks are tricky for them to take
D ad and me think Liverpool are great.

David Mellor (12)
Ryles Park High School

Trees

An autumn's day
In late October
The weather is
Sunny and fresh
I am walking along
Flying my kite
It gets caught in the wind
And stuck in the tree
Red, orange, brown
Yellow and golden
The leaves are falling
On my head
Whistling and rustling
Blowing and swaying
The noises I heard
On this blustery day.

Sarah Buckley (13)
Ryles Park High School

The Forest

Wet, damp, scary forest at night,
Eyes looking at you from every direction,
Crackling sticks, howls getting closer and closer,
The wind whistling at you,
Echoing all around,
You can hear leaves crunching like bone,
Scared to close your eyes,
Seeing shadows, hearing nails scratching on the trees,
You're wet and cold,
All alone.

Jake Cotterill (12)
Ryles Park High School

Cats

Cats moan
Cats groan
Some always moan
They eat and sleep
And they always peep
I love my cat
Pretty and white
It isn't fair
If they're
Tabby and tight.

Casey Harrison (12)
Ryles Park High School

The Spooky House

There was a really spooky house
Trees were surrounding it and
They were waving
And red and brown and light yellow leaves fell down
And something echoed across the trees
It was very spooky
And cold.

Amy Curley (12)
Ryles Park High School

The Haunted House

A haunted house stood on a hill,
I went for a walk after watching The Bill,
I could hear chains clanging
And loads of doors banging,
The house was in the dark mist,
I was stood there shivering like a kid.

Tasha Clowes (12)
Ryles Park High School

The Journey Of Imagination

Take me on a journey
Of spectacular madness and invincible hopes
I want to see all colours of the sun
That casts all loving lights onto my watery eyes
Take me to the symposium of laughter
And we can all laugh until our heads quite literally fall off
I want to see death being carted away
By the men in authoritative blue
How that would be amusing to the senses
I don't like the colour of the sea
So let's change it to an uplifting yellow
Watch the moon crack open
And out shall spill a golden yolk
Get rid of the eclipse within
And let the light spill out into the melancholy airwaves
My saurian-like eyes are eager to explode whilst wanting to implode
Leave behind your dull pride
Just break out into a frenzied state of happiness
Imagine the trees growing taller and dancing in the wind
Watch the stars leap out of the sea
And orbit rapidly around your large head
Numb feet can't carry me up the stairs
See the rainbow spring up out of the void wasteland
City life dull and short-lived
Get rid of the old towering city and in its place
Place a Hispanic hippopotamus
Imagine Dionysus handing out bottles of mouth-watering wine
And Aphrodite dancing on the roof of the Christian church
Go swim with the fish that wear dazzling colours of a painter's dream
Who cares what may happen
It's an epic journey taking you to the very edge of your senses.

Wayne Woodward (14)
Ryles Park High School

Cats

Cats are black
Or any colour
They always are so nice
They miaow when they want to come in
Or when they want to be fed
Or when they want to be let out.

Erin Brooks (14)
Ryles Park High School

My Poem

People walking through a dark forest
Leaves rustling
Wind rustling
You're all alone
And then
Suddenly
There's a big
Scream!

Daniel Burns (12)
Ryles Park High School

The Red Car

Wheels turn,
Like a rocket,
The red car goes
Like the wind,
The red car goes
Fast as a train,
The red car goes.

Christopher Douglas (12)
Ryles Park High School

The Stars

The stars twinkle in the sky at night,
They look nice at night in the sky,
The stars light up the sky like diamonds,
The stars look like they are staring at you,
The stars look like they are so close to the Earth,
They are so super that they make me happy,
When the stars are feeling dizzy,
The stars look like they have a face on them,
The stars took a man off Earth and put him on top of them.

Christopher Huxley (13)
Ryles Park High School

Rivers

River flowing calmly,
Clean and fresh,
Little waves rippling,
Shining in the sun,
Slowly, peacefully, meandering,
Then suddenly it gets faster,
It drops down a waterfall
And ends up in a pool.

Hannah Lee (13)
Ryles Park High School

Cat

The cat sneaks down on all fours
She preys on the ball of wool

Then she delicately washes herself clean

She licks her paws and gently cleans her whiskers

She cuddles up in her fluffy bed
And softly swishes her tail.

Rebecca Whitehurst (14)
Ryles Park High School

There Goes My Fishing Rod

As I come to the bank
I put down my box
I pull out my rod and also my hooks
Throw in my keep-net
The maggots are turning
I cast out so far
I wait and I wait
But no fish are biting
The float moves at last
Is it a nibble or is it a bite?
It is a perch or is it a pike?
Reel in my line, I gaze the float
I notice out far
A small canal boat
There goes my rod
There goes my line
What about the carp?
I thought it was mine.

Gavin Murphy (13)
Ryles Park High School

The Dog

The dog has a bone
He munches and crunches
His mouth goes, is excited
The dog's tail
Whisks and frisks
His tail goes

The dog goes after a cat
Fast as fast
His legs go.

Harry Taylor (13)
Ryles Park High School

All About Mrs Ryan

This is all about Mrs Ryan
The sweetest teacher here
Here is a list of what we can think of her

Nice, kind, understanding, sweet,
Somebody who listens, nice to talk to, funny.

Mrs Ryan likes her pets,
She has got a bulldog,
She thinks it's very sweet,
The whole of her class thinks she is very sweet.

Mrs Ryan is a laugh
She jokes with us in the class

This is the poem about the teacher
That has the best laugh.

Kayliegh Rowe & Stacey Brown (13)
Ryles Park High School

Horses

The horse is good,
Horses have nice colours
An can run fast
In a field
When horses gallop
It's horses, horses
Around on the ground.

Christine Postlewhite (12)
Ryles Park High School

The Wind

The wind blows the leaves
Gently across the road
The bushes sway
From side to side

The wind howls
Through gaps in the window
It makes me
Shiver, shiver, shiver

The wind can be strong
To make a tree fall down
The wind blows
The wind howls.

Stuart Reid (13)
Ryles Park High School

Butterfly

A butterfly flaps its wings
Very fast
The wings speed
The butterfly wings
Flutter and beat
The butterfly makes its way
Onto a sunflower
Yellow, round like the sun
It drinks the nectar
Out of the flower
Sucking it into its mouth.

Nicole Weaver (13)
Ryles Park High School

The Forest

Walking through the forest is always fun,
Seeing all kinds of creatures run

Crunching leaves here and there
Look at the trees, they are so bare

Lots of pine cones have dropped
Look at that rabbit with its ears cropped

There's something in that bush
Everybody let's hush

Oh look, it's a fox
With gleaming white socks

Now I am at the end of the track
With the moonlight shining on my back.

Charlotte Crooks (12)
Ryles Park High School

My Best Friend, Maddie

Watch Maddie as she plays with me
Like a sister she'll always be

She's a faithful friend and loyal too
I'll always protect her like big brothers do

She's very spotty, more black than white
She moults all the time like lines of thin white

She's nimble for flies, for spiders she's fast
Chasing spiders is tiring - she wobbles to sleep at last

Attention is what she loves at rest
A Dalmatian is what she is and she's the best.

Dale Sullivan (14)
Ryles Park High School

My Cat, Felix

Felix, my cat
Is as soft as a mat
And she likes to eat and chase the rats

She is so cute
She walks around sniffing your boots

She will do you no harm
All she does is lick your arm

She purrs all day
She purrs all night
She is waiting at your door
And wakes up all right.

Simon Walker (13)
Ryles Park High School

Rabbits And Foxes

Rabbits jump all day long
Gallop through the snow
Scratches hard through the snow
To try and find some grass
Then the fox creeps up and makes
The rabbit run away in a dash.

Kimberley Huxley (12)
Ryles Park High School

The Redcoat Diaries

The sky was made of ebony, the moon rested tonight,
Although the stars were gone, the flames of our torches shone bright.
The wood leered up against us oh, formidable woods in the darkness,
And we touched the unchartered trees in the blackness; who stood up
Straight and still, and whose depth concealed the armed highwaymen,
Samuel and Steel.

Through we tramped, through grass, mud and water,
Though we were strong we began to saunter.
We made our guns ready, the fire prepared
And as we went to bed that night I knew we were all scared,
For when we abandoned ourselves to sleep, the same sound we
all heard.

Ere the dawn we awoke, but we had a shock to see;
As instead of our company being a strong five we only had
a measly three!
Far we searched in all directions, but all in vain
For as we crossed the river, we saw two familiar faces again.

Now we advanced with caution for we knew what hid in the woods,
Along with a box of tea, some china and who knows what other kinds
of goods.
This was our final test, but our bounty was good.
We crept cautiously along this mud, for we knew we must avenge
our friends' split blood.

We made camp tonight, my friends on guard duty, while I
(lazy lummox)
Just slept tight.

I woke in the night to see such a fright; my friends lay dead by the fire.
I had no help to give them, I could have saved them.
I suddenly felt a cold and incredible pain in my back
Of leaking blood I felt no lack.
But as I twisted and turned, I felt another hack.
I looked round in the darkness and saw a glint of *steel!*
Quick as a flash I drew my musket, I fired there and then, I did that
for all,
Save myself; poor dying Paul.

George Massey (11)
St Ambrose College, Altrincham

The Match

My hobby is lacrosse
It's very, very fun
If you don't like it, it's your loss
It really makes you run

We play it in the winter
And when we run to the huddle
Nelly, who's our coach
Is standing in a puddle

We started the new quarter
Weaving in and out
We hope it would be a slaughter
That's what we said in the shout

The final whistle came
We went to the club
At last! Out of the rain
I wished I was the sub.

We tried our best
To win, so plucky
It's a fact
4-3 was lucky.

Robert Edwards (11)
St Ambrose College, Altrincham

My School Dinners!

The chips are unbearable,
They're torture to eat,
They smell like my dad's dirty old feet.
The gravy's thick, it makes me wanna be sick.
The peas are bright green and not to be seen!
The pizzas are cheesy,
They make me feel queasy,
The sausages are torpedoes,
This is what I wish that they would blow up
And make a new dish!

Ben Magill (12)
St Ambrose College, Altrincham

Yeah, Whatever

Hello bully, long time no see,
Did you have a nice summer?
Did you miss bullying me?
I'm feeing stronger now,
Ready for your hurtful ways,
You don't frighten me anymore,
With the cruel things you say.
You've got your own problems,
I could bet,
Because while you're bullying me,
No one's bullying you . . . *yet*.
If I turn away,
You can't see,
Just how much you're hurting me,
For both our sakes in the end,
Rather than be my bully,
Wouldn't it be better
To be my friend?
You bully all the small kids,
Do you think that's clever?
So you think you're the big guy,
Yeah, whatever.

Sean Wright (11)
St Ambrose College, Altrincham

Rugby

Rugby is full of surprises
And loads of different laws,
Like running at them,
When they're taking a pen
And fighting over who's getting the ball.

Nicholas Henry (11)
St Ambrose College, Altrincham

An Ordinary Day

He wakes up early, not very fun,
His eyes are tortured by the sun.
Eating cereal, not very nice,
Tastes like it's been licked by mice.
Got to get the bus, can't be late,
But he can't get past the front gate.
He wasn't late and didn't miss the bus,
Even with all that fuss.
Got to school, made it alive,
He didn't think he would survive.
Into the classroom he will go,
Will he make it? I don't think so.
Another teacher shouts,
What is he on about?
Forgot his homework again,
He made a lie,
Apparently his grandma died.
He didn't believe him,
He said Grandma already died last weekend,
So he got detention,
Went home a bored and tired person.
Did his homework,
Until he could say a perk,
Now he lay with a comfortable body
And a comfortable head,
The best place in the world
Is his bed.

Aaron Ward (12)
St Ambrose College, Altrincham

My Favourite Footie Team

Footie is a very good game,
Of course you've got to know your team's name.
I think van Nistelrooy is the best,
That's why I've got him on my vest.
Man United is my team,
So when you think you're winning, it's just a dream.
Man United are the best,
That's why they had players like George Best.
United are in the Premiership,
So let me give you a tip,
If your team is playing them,
Remember we're one in a million
And we're gonna thrash them again and again.

Martin Solomon (11)
St Ambrose College, Altrincham

The Rugby World Cup

The rugby world cup is a fascinating thing
My dad and my grandpa just sit there watching
Now it's begun, they never want it to end
I sit there thinking it must be the new trend

The suspense, the excitement, the skill
These things make watchers attentive
But of course . . . tickets are expensive!

In two months it will come to an end
The craze will be over and so will the trend
Now what will my dad and grandpa do?
I think they'll find some more rugby, do you?

Joseph Cooper (11)
St Ambrose College, Altrincham

Just Helping A Friend

I woke up in a hurry,
My mum was in a flurry,
I got ready for school
And made my hair look cool.

I had to run for the bus,
Because my mum had made such a fuss,
I saw my best friend, Tim,
Something seemed to be wrong with him.

I thought we'd chill out and chat,
To talk about this and that,
Because to get things off your chest,
Talking to your mate's the best.

The next day I saw him with a smile,
So our chat seemed to have been worthwhile,
So what had I achieved in the end
Was to help a good friend.

Daniel Gunn (11)
St Ambrose College, Altrincham

My Acrostic Poem

M y family is the best, we're definitely cooler than all the rest
Y is for the cool colour yellow, my sister's hobby is playing the cello

F is for family, also known as similarity
A nnoying is my sister, don't know how I can kiss her
M y sister's scared of monsters, I think she's going bonkers
I is for I love my family, especially when they're really kind to me
L oving is my mum and dad, when they're around things
                                              are never bad
Y awning is my family's hobby; we're always sleepy just like Corrie.

Alex Waterhouse (11)
St Ambrose College, Altrincham

Skateboarding

S is for skateboard, which you need to skate
K is for kickflip, to do may take a long wait
A is for airwalk, a dangerous trick to do
T is for tailslide, when done, will thrill you!
E is for Enjoi, a good skateboard make
B is for backflip, from which your life could be at stake!
O is for *ouch!* Which skating will cause!
A is for air, when big needs applause!
R is for rail, a good object to grind
D is for darkslide, a trick which is hard to find
I is for indy, an easy trick for pros
N is for nollie-flip, a trick that just flows!
G is for great, which skateboarding is
    it also takes courage, so overcome your fears!

Tom Gurrie (11)
St Ambrose College, Altrincham

My Mad Dog

Have you got a mad dog?
Just like me,
Is your mad dog
A he or a she?

My dog's a he,
Just like me,
Does your dog mark their territory?

My dog's a Boxer
And energy he's lots-a!
My dog is mad
But hardly ever sad!

Have you got a mad dog just like me?

Aaron Gibbons (12)
St Ambrose College, Altrincham

Christian Hickson

C alling all who want to listen,
H ere is a story about my world.
R ight at the start,
I was born in Wythenshawe.
S ale is where I live,
T here is me, my mum and my dad,
I wish I had a brother.
A t weekends I practice my music,
N ot only piano but saxophone as well.

H olidays I spend in Tenerife,
I t's very hot and sunny,
C omputer games and reading are my hobbies,
K ittens, I have two,
S uch good fun they are,
O ut of the two I like the boy best,
N ow it is time to go.

Christian Hickson (11)
St Ambrose College, Altrincham

A Monster

M ean monstrous monster
O dious, odorous, obscene
N asty, nightmarish, neutralising
S melly, strong, striking
T all, terrible, teeth
E nraged, enormous, emphatic
R oaring, raging, rioting.

Mark Arnfield (11)
St Ambrose College, Altrincham

Escape From The Zoo

A day at the zoo couldn't get worse, and
I'm going to tell you about it in verse

The animals have escaped from the zoo
And the keepers don't know what to do!

The chimps swing like gymnasts in the big top,
While the kangaroos speed away in a hoop.
The snakes slither under the gate,
Escaping from the food they hate.

The giraffe lolloping along with its elegant neck,
Checking out trees and leaves on its trek.
Not far above, the dark bats fly next to the colour-washed parrots,
While the goats savagely eat the grocer's carrots.

The tiger walked daringly down the street,
Raiding the butchers of all their meat.
The big brown bear with its long wavy hair,
Growling and prowling, hunting for its lair.

As if nothing had happened the sloth soundly slept,
While below him the keepers wailed and wept.

James Carr (11)
St Ambrose College, Altrincham

Rugby Is A Game For The Rough

R ugby is a game for the rough
U nhealthy people just aren't tough enough
G rab him by the legs and take him down
B oys beware the mud'll turn you brown
Y ou might come off the pitch with a dirty frown.

Alex Hartley (11)
St Ambrose College, Altrincham

The Monster

There's a monster under my bed,
It's scaring me at night,
I don't know what to do, or where to go,
I just know it's up for a fight.

I'm too scared to go under and look,
I need to put on a brave face,
Whenever I have the chance to go down,
I just know it will snap my brace.

I am ready for it now,
I'm going to go under and look,
I've got the right equipment and I'm not scared,
I've also brought a monster book.

I'm underneath my bed,
It's all dark, gloomy and weird,
Just then I heard a creak,
That little boy disappeared.

Matthew Baker (11)
St Ambrose College, Altrincham

Football

F ootball can be played anywhere at any time.
O verall it is the most popular sport in the world.
O ffside is a very important rule of the game.
T ackling, technique and tenacity are three good aspects
   of the game.
B oth teams start a match with 11 players,
A ll matches are 90 minutes long including half-time at 45 minutes.
L ots of teams from inside Europe participate in the Champions
   League, a huge tournament that only the best team wins.
L oving and living football are my priorities.

James Taberham (12)
St Ambrose College, Altrincham

My Cat

My kitten is called Amber,
she runs up the stairs and
climbs up the walls,
the paper it tears.
She plays with my keys and
my toys they make a noise.
She sleeps all the day
And runs wild at night.
She runs around to attack the mice,
She is very nice.
With her sharp teeth she bites,
I will give her a fright.
She cries for her dinner,
She cries for her tea,
Oh when is my mummy going to feed me?
She's got sharp claws on her paws
And she opens the doors.
She's cuddly, nice and lovely to hold
But where there are dogs, she's not very bold.
So isn't it nice like a cat to be free,
That's the end of the poem
And the story is told.

Marek Walker (11)
St Ambrose College, Altrincham

At The Front

S hells flying past like demons from above.
O nly fools and madmen cross the deadly wire.
L iving six feet under although walking about.
D ying men all around.
I nevitable that more men will meet their end.
E veryone scared stiff waiting for the whistle to blow.
R emembering my friends so dear who lost their lives
    so tragically here.

Thomas Appleton (11)
St Ambrose College, Altrincham

Prisoner Of Rhythm

Headphones firmly clamped,
Volume on full blast,
The switch was flicked,
His mind was braced
And then at long, long last . . .

The music filled his ears,
Like cement into a hole.
The beat carried on,
As he broke into song,
Then the tune reached its musical goal.

He was now in a musical haven,
The tune, filtering through his mind.
Quavers and clefs,
Whizzing past his eyes,
As he drifted out of time.

His mind, a prisoner of rhythm,
His ears, the bars of the cell,
The climax neared
And as he feared,
The end was close as well.

The speed of the music decreased,
Sadly, he would soon be free
Of that wonderful song
And then, it seemed so wrong,
The music ceased to be.

Dan Cere (12)
St Ambrose College, Altrincham

Teacher Features

Mr Gwyer sings in the school choir.
Mrs Gunning is always running.
Mr Thwaite uses weights.
Mrs Kendry is very friendly.
Mr Lewis loves to eat Chewits.

Ryan Moffatt (12)
St Ambrose College, Altrincham

Once Upon A Time . . .

Once upon a time in a faraway land,
Lived a king and a queen,
True love they had found.

Life was so simple till suddenly it hit,
Why did they have a giant muck pit?

The smell was so bad,
Worse than the King's BO,
The Queen called her servants and
Said it had to go.

Move it from my garden
Or you'll all lose your job,
Send it to the farmer,
The one called Bob.

So off it was sent to the farmer called Bob
And no one ever did lose their job.

Vicky Armstrong (13)
Tarporley Community High School

Birdman

The sad birdman makes his call,
All around the dark, empty hall.
If he sees a robin,
He will ride it till it's throbbin'.
When he sees a blue tit in the med,
He would slice off it's lovely head.
He has an ugly, fat wife,
So he stabbed himself with a 10 inch knife.
When his wife found out,
She cried like a trout.
Then she lost some weight
And turned into a really attractive mate.
Poor, poor, poor Paul,
Now Paul is very *sad!*
Too bad!

George White (12)
Tarporley Community High School

A Traumatic Moment

Crash!
Sudden movements,
Heartless shouts,
Dullness all around,
Compact spaces,
Scary jolts,
'We're sinking down, down, down.'

Cold, dark waters,
Killer sharks,
People slipping overboard,
Disaster's struck,
'We're out of luck,'
Shriek terrified voices all around.

Horror-struck people,
Icy water,
A jolt from down below,
The people shout,
The boat has ceased,
With luck we may survive.

Lois Walley (12)
Tarporley Community High School

Teachers

Teachers, teachers how boring are they?
It's nothing but tests and lectures all day,
Who gives us good educational fun,
It's also good if I could just say,
Don't ever trust a teacher in any school again.
They never shut up and are all so loud,
If they could just shut up I'd be so awfully proud.

Daniel Hopwood (12)
Tarporley Community High School

My World

I'm on a beach,
What do I see?
Blue waters flowing in front of me
And dolphins frolicking in the sea.

I'm in the country,
What do I see?
Trees covering me from all around
And birds making little sound.

I'm in the mountainside,
What do I see?
A beautiful view round and round
And snow covering my feet and the ground.

I'm in the dark,
What do I see?
No view, no animal,
Nothing, nothing at all.

How lucky we are to see these things,
As well as being able to hear and sing.
How I love the world we are in,
Land and water, people within.

Jess Brownlee (13)
Tarporley Community High School

Follow No One

What drives a man to dream of wide open spaces?
To work the land until the light of day is gone?
To beat the sun to that perfect spot in the woods?
It is the basic ideal shared by every pioneer,
To follow no one!

Alexander Gittins (12)
Tarporley Community High School

Santa

Santa came riding
In his sleigh so high,
Over the world
Up in the sky.

Pulled by reindeer
Going really fast,
The children were snoring
As he flew past.

Santa came down the chimney
And sat with a plop,
He needed a rest because
He had so many presents to drop.

Santa came quietly
And slowly opened the door,
Then he silently placed
The presents on the floor.

The adults said
'Shut your eyes tight,
Then Santa will deliver
Your presents in the night.'

In the morning
The children said, 'Yey.'
They opened their presents
All through the day.

Richard Pover (12)
Tarporley Community High School

My World

Where clouds are white as cornflakes
And sky is blue as grass,
Raindrops big as boulders,
Fall all over the grass.

Hippos here can fly,
People here can soar,
They don't take any chances,
They fly through open doors.

Where friends don't ever fall out
And everything's forever,
Nothing bad ever happens,
Everyone's together.

If only my world was real,
Maybe murder wouldn't be,
Then people would still be here,
Everyone be free.

Georgina Dotchin (12)
Tarporley Community High School

The Volcano

The volcano is a humble thing,
A bit like a jack-in-the-box,
It sits and sits and waits and waits,
Until it has been wound up enough by its volcanic gas.
It is then ready to show its true colours,
It starts slow just like a flower would,
But then it goes for it with colour with all its might.
With fire and brimstone and smoke and ash,
It burns and burns for all to see.
Its mighty colours burning bright,
But then it starts to burn away.
No longer having all that power,
Just like a flower would.

David Barden (12)
Tarporley Community High School

My Poem

In this valley all dark and gloomed,
Lie bodies of men who have conquered and killed
And for 90 years in the freezing cold,
These bodies of men lay out all dead,
But remember that although they died,
In the foreign moon freezing at night,
A corner of this foreign field shall always be proud
And British and partly mine
And for that those men died,
Cold, alone but fighting on,
For king and country and to die a cold death
At the enemy's bomb.

David Clarke (12)
Tarporley Community High School

Identity

I am hot and cold
Timid, though bold
I am evil, yet good
I am crouched and stood

I am the hooded creature
I have the eyes of eagle, ears of a fox
I am as heavy as an elephant and as light as a paper box
I am clumsy, yet agile

I have a body of a cute fluffy squirrel,
But a soul of pure evil.

Ryder Caldwell (12)
Tarporley Community High School

Senses

The sight I see
The place I am
The beauty of the scene

A sunset on a sea so clean
A newborn lamb bounding round a green

The eagle flying overhead
A mole right underneath

The sounds I hear
The animals I touch
It's gone, it's gone away.

Rachel O'Neill (12)
Tarporley Community High School

My Pony

I know a pony,
You can see him, he's lonely,
He needs a friend,
His love will never end.
His body is brown,
With four white feet,
He whinnies every time we meet,
His mane and tail are grey,
I wish he could stay.
He loves to jump and gallop around,
So all you can hear is the thud from the ground.
I love the way he prances around and around.

Holly Davies (12)
Tarporley Community High School

Life And Its Troubles

Life is hard if you never stop and think,
So just stop, put your feet up and relax,
You must never work over the max,
Things never go as planned.
Life may seem like an obstacle course,
But don't rush like a racehorse,
You have days that are dark and sad,
You will get through it if you don't get mad.

Life and its troubles,
In life you have to be prepared,
So that you don't get scared.
No matter what life throws at you,
You will always have someone to turn to.

You will have good days and bad days,
But I will be there always!

Jessica Craven (12)
Tarporley Community High School

The Ghost In My Room

Alone in my bed I lay,
As I cuddle my pillow to keep them away.

But I'm sure something's there,
As someone touches and strokes my hair.

I get up, look round my room, then go back to bed,
Whilst I try to persuade myself more like the shed.

They spook me out in the middle of the night,
So I sit up, scream, switch on the light.

Surprisingly I feel at ease,
Don't hurt me if I please.

Goodnight I say,
I lay there and pray.

Eleanor Cheeseman (12)
Tarporley Community High School

Our World

What is going on in our world?
Why do we cut down the trees?
Why do animals lose their home because we cut trees?
What do you think how they feel?
Would they be scared and it is unfair that they have to move
How would you feel if you lost your home?
Why do we do it to them?
At the end of the day, they are humans like you and me.

Why do we cut down trees so we can put up houses
Or put up workplaces?
We should get a place where trees are not cut down
And animals have a place to stay.

Rachel Glover (12)
Tarporley Community High School

Italy

Italy is the nicest place, my number one inside!
Forget Spain, France, America, Australia and 'Thai'!
It has the most beautiful cities,
Milan, Venice, Verona and Sicily!
As the sun beats down on you,
You wipe your brow with a tissue!
When you arrive at Luton airport,
Your memories come back to haunt!

Myles Carr (12)
Tarporley Community High School

Spiders!

They come from the strangest places
And scare so many faces
They crawl anywhere they can
Just to get to their one man
The sight of it gets you trembling
While they are assembling their little friends
So you take the step and face your fear
As the truth draws near!
Then squelch and it is dead
The spider is no longer the fear in your head!

Toni Burton (12)
Tarporley Community High School

Envy

I am a feeling that can lead to death
I lurk around but have no breath

I hide in the dark and wait for prey
And come alive at the break of day

And when you think I have retired
I'll turn around and call Desire

I make you want what they have got
To look around and want the lot

But in the end just sit alone
And worry about what you don't own.

Jacob Hall (12)
Tarporley Community High School

My Fear

As I stand my rifle in my arms
My friend beside me uttering holy psalms
The wind lashing me in the face
Wondering why I'm in this place
These trenches filled with muck and dirt
Soldiers scared, dead or hurt
No one here can say they're not scared
Between us the fear is shared

Standing here wanting to cry
The others believing they're going to die
Knowing soon we're off to fight
Mass murder in the dead of night
Climbing up the ladder to war
Now I know what I'm fighting for
Guns firing, mines explode
Everyone's mind on killing mode
Somehow I know my death is near
Yes, yes, the end is here.

Stephen Jennings (12)
Tarporley Community High School

I Wonder Who?

Who made penguins?
Wouldn't you like to know
They forgot to give them knees
I've always wanted to know why
They've never freezed
I wonder if they are full of antifreeze?

Who made rabbits?
Wouldn't you like to know
I'll tell you why
To teach us all
How to multiply.

Jonty Deynem (12)
Tarporley Community High School

The Seasons

Spring

Spring is when people sing,
As we hear the wedding bells ring,
Spring is a season in-between,
But not everyone's so keen.

Summer

Yellow and red,
As I look at the sun from my bed,
The morning is here,
As we fish on the pier.

Autumn

Red, brown, golden leaves,
Falling and swaying of golden trees,
As people rake them into piles,
Bare trees go on for miles.

Winter

Blue and white all day and night,
Now it's morning, the nights are boring,
The street lights get bolder,
As it gets colder.

Stacey Munro (12)
Tarporley Community High School

My Shadow

I have a shadow that goes everywhere with me
What could be the use for him is more than I can see
He's very, very like me from my heels up to my head
And I see him jump before me as I jump onto my bed
He sometimes shoots up taller like a bouncing rubber ball
And he sometimes gets so little you can't see him at all.

Bethany Andrew (12)
Tarporley Community High School

I Am With You

When you kiss me goodnight
I whisper 'I love you'
I know tonight I will be safe
Because I am with you

When you wake me up in the morning
You say 'Good morning sleepyhead!'
I know today we will have fun
Because I am with you

Then one day you went away
I never saw you again
No one to kiss me goodnight
No one to keep me safe

Lonely I go to bed
Turn off the light
And in the darkness
I hear a voice
It says 'I love you'

I know now that I am safe
I know I won't be harmed
Because I am with you
You are in my heart.

Laura Rourke (13)
Tarporley Community High School

Holiday

In the seasons of Spain,
There can be a pain,
The weather changing one to another,
It's really a bother,
You go on holiday with your mum, dad and brother,
Your brother's a bother, oh dear, oh dear, oh bother.

Eric Jones (12)
Tarporley Community High School

Home/School

A house cold, hard, no warmth to it,
The edges, the colour of the night sky,
Outside peace is spared.

The children screaming, can't find their things,
Mothers worry, frantic about work.

School's open, children flood in.

Birds fly past with an open eye.

Children run,
Dropping litter.

Teachers worry, frantic expressions, gloomy.

Hard headmaster strolls towards staffroom.

The assembly hushed, headmaster walks through,
Children cough to annoy headmaster.

Silence is sweet but doesn't last long,
No noise is heard.

Kelly Wynne (15)
Tarporley Community High School

Winter

Snow twirling round and round,
Like white feathers falling to the ground.
Landing silently beneath my feet,
I look up at the snowy sky,
White as a pearly ghost.

As I walk through the pure white sheet,
It crunches beneath my feet.
My footprints become engraved,
Until more snow lands
And falls into their place.

Sarah Mills (13)
Tarporley Community High School

Wedding Day

The birds were singing
And the bells were ringing,
'It must be a wedding,' my friend said to me,
'Shall we go have a look?'
At the church by the brook,
We'll have to be quick,
To see our new vicar,
If we don't leave now,
We will have to run much quicker.

Here comes the bride,
With her groom by her side,
Her carriage awaits,
Down by the church gates,
The presents are given,
The cake has been cut,
The guests are all waiting,
With smiles on their faces,
To throw the confetti
And wish them good luck.

They left that day,
For the sun and the sand,
They walked on the beach hand in hand,
Under the moonlight as they kissed goodnight,
They pledged their love for one another,
Then they went to their hotel
And had tea and supper.

Zara Welch (12)
Tarporley Community High School

Alpha-Class

A is for Anna who sits on a stool,
B is for Bernard who is really cruel,
C is for Cherry who stands on her head,
D is for David who stays in bed,
E is for Ellen who is really loud,
F is for Faye who hangs with the crowd,
G is for Gordon who bosses around,
H is for Hannah who watches TV,
I is for Ingrid who thinks he's a bee,
J is for Jack who loves to read books,
K is for Katy who has no looks,
L is for Liam who loves to eat,
M is for Malcolm who has big feet,
N is for Nikki who swims all day,
O is for Oscar who loves to play,
P is for Pippa who loves her hair,
Q is for Quincy who likes teddy bears,
R is for Richard who climbs trees,
S is for Sarah who has wobbly knees,
T is for Tommy who eats lots of sweets,
U is for Ursula who has a shirt full of pleats,
V is for Viria who is very jolly,
W is for Will who owns a bright pink brolly,
X is for Xena who is all vain,
Y is for Yasmin who loves to play games,
Z is for Zara and that is my name.

Charlotte Lister (12)
Tarporley Community High School

Treasures

Treasures are things that are special
Treasures are things to keep safe
Treasures are things to cherish forever
Remember to keep them in place

Treasures are coins and spoons
Treasures are photos and cards
Treasures are letters and gifts
Remember to always safeguard

Never forget all your treasures
Never forget what they're worth
Your children will always remember
Your treasures begin at birth.

Cherry Swift (12)
Tarporley Community High School

Sunset

It appears like a ripened apple
And disappears into the sky,
Its rays glisten on the beautiful blue sea,
People stop and stare,
Just like a gormless young child.

Its beautiful colours reflect off people's sunglasses,
It expands across the land showing off its glory
It amazes people all over the world,
Like a quiet class of children.

Its beautiful sight gives it a reputation,
Of being a beautiful thing in our nation,
It stops people in the streets
And brings people in fleets.

Hannah Aftab (12)
Tarporley Community High School

Sleepless Nights

She was full of hate,
A danger to near and far,
As the breeze smothered her narrow body in guilt,
She expressed a heavy sigh and thought.

She wanted to let go,
To everything she had and that they would drift away.

She was full of sorrow, yet she was not stressed nor scared,
Drifting she was, not to be missed, in this sick, none-caring world.

She was trapped inside her own doings,
Feeling claustrophobia coming through her twisted mind,
She felt like a puppet, tied with strings
And those strings were knotted and tangled.

She closed her eyes and dreamed of the future,
The crying, the killing,
All she was now getting away from.

Wake up, she thought
And with one regretting push of might,
She got to breathe again.

She wasn't sure why,
But she was crying,
Of water and tears,
Of stress and concern,
Of life.

She chose to get away from this world
And thus she almost succeeded,
She wanted just for once some joy,
So she took the winding path called destiny
And then, she vanished.

David Worrall (12)
Tarporley Community High School

All Alone

It was a cold day, a hot night,
He was always scared, all alone.
He only had an imaginary friend,
Though he was never there now.
On the bus he didn't talk,
At school he sat on his own,
At lunch he was always alone,
When he got home he didn't speak,
Before his tea he cried,
Then there was a knock on the door,
It was a child asking for help,
Another little boy wanted to play,
Immediately the answer was yes!

Nathan Seeney (12)
Tarporley Community High School

Water

It's running away,
Down, down the mountain,
Escaping,
Pouring over ledges,
Cascading between the rocks,
Rushing along,
Racing along,
It's going to reach the bottom
And then it slows,
Slows right down,
Narrows,
Disappears,
Into the darkness,
Underground.

Sarah Chynoweth (14)
Tarporley Community High School

The Secret

The secret is a whisper, a word, a note,
Ink on blotting paper it spreads,
Interlinking circles, a chain of secrets.
Always moving never stopping,
Round and round and round and round,
Swift, cutting through the boring everyday chat,
Homing in on its next target,
Circling round,
Whilst,
Overflowing pools of whispers tip and stream into the next,
Unknown words pass behind people's backs,
The secret rears and halts at a crossroad,
Spiralling back on itself until,
It's overtaken and falls behind,
The growing wake of a new fugitive,
A new stone's ripples shake the pool of whispers
And the sequence starts all over again.

Jocelyn Little (14)
Tarporley Community High School

Outdoor PE

They assemble outside the aged double doors
Like lambs to the slaughter
They huddle together like penguins in Arctic conditions
The frost invades their football boots with bitter cold
Their strict uniform allows the cold air in from all angles

The PE teacher ambles around the corner with his steaming
Mug of coffee that strikes jealousy into the boy's eyes
The mumbling dies as the presence of the teacher arrives
Like the condensation in the air that is hovering over the group
Their destination is reached, it's a moral victory they survived.

Graham Dodd (15)
Tarporley Community High School

Kes

Silence
The flap of the wings
Still silence
The hawk bores down
Silence

'Come on Kes!'
The boy cries
Swinging the lure like a lasso
The hawk swoops
Missed

'Come one Kes!'
Cries the boy again
The lure still swinging like a merry-go-round
The hawk hangs in the air, swoops
Misses

'Last time Kes!'
The call from the boy
The hawk circles like a fighter jet
Speeds, swoops, talons ready
The beef snatched from the lure

'Good girl, Kes!'
The boy congratulates the hawk
The beef torn to pieces
The hawk eats
Victory!

Phil Johnson (15)
Tarporley Community High School

Bullies

A line of faces,
Hard edged, faded,
Huddled together like ravenous vultures,
Picking on the rotten meat of my despair.

A line of faces,
Mouths open, spewing poison,
Burning my face, arms, body,
Eyes morphing into black holes.

A line of faces,
Block the sun,
Standing like tombstones,
Sapping my last hopes.

A line of faces,
Punching, kicking.

A line of faces,
Then,
Darkness.

Nicola Jeffrey (16)
Tarporley Community High School

Billy

Billy a boy,
So weak and frail,
Warm-hearted and wanting love,
Sits all alone with Kes elegantly perched on his arm,
Billy so scared waiting for Jud,
He stands,
You can just see skin and bones,
Eyes like golf balls sitting in their sockets,
Dirty marks smother his face,
Billy's soul locked away longing to be released.

Anna Holden (15)
Tarporley Community High School

Kes

One wing opened like a fan,
Swooping for its prey,
Its voice too soft to be heard,
'Kes,' shouted a young boy,
Her claws gripped the glove,
Eating her meat.

Her eyes looked threatening
As she flew high over ground,
Up and down like a yo-yo,
Not a scrap of beef distracts her
As she completes a circuit.

The beef too low for her attack,
As she circles the young boy so innocent watching,
She swoops, wings in and gradually hits her target,
An audience clapped at the sight.

Becky Winward (15)
Tarporley Community High School

A Poem Of A Line

The line came down with
A hawk and a crack
A splitting smack
An ear-breaking noise
The rattle and the snap
As the knuckles contract
And crunch together
Like the clap of
Thunder as they clash
Upon one another.

Benjamin Corbett-Mills (15)
Tarporley Community High School

The Hawk

The hawk flies through the air,
It glides like a plane,
It is quick, like a cheetah
And its flight drives you insane.

A hawk is a bird,
It watches its prey
And when it's caught it,
It likes to play.

When the hawk flies,
It makes you wonder,
Its flight's distinctive,
Similar to thunder.

A hawk is different
Than any other bird,
Because when it glides,
It can't be heard.

Matthew Jones (15)
Tarporley Community High School

F1

The shimmering glisten on the F1 cars,
The deafening noise of the roaring engine,
As they line up like a queue of shopping trolleys,
The shimmering line of the horizon of the heat,
The grey smoke rises as they leave the starts,
Round the dust track, the rubber all over the track,
Then as he crosses the white chequered line
The crowd roar.

Jack Page (12)
Tarporley Community High School

Billy

The alarm clock rings
The boy arises
Down in the dark, gloomy room
Doing the jobs around the house
Finding there is no food

No love is shown to the boy
Not even by his mum or brother
What sort of family is this?
It makes you wonder

But when his life is changed
Silence overcomes him
Watching a beautiful animal
Swooping around the area

The bird his only friend
The only one who listens.

Samantha Parker (15)
Tarporley Community High School

Kes

The moment comes,
Billy walks through the woods.
The sticks and leaves crack like a packet of crisps.

The wind picks up,
The trees whistle in the wind,
Like a group of birds.

Kes looks up at Billy.

Love at first sight,
Billy spent all his time rearing his bird.

She is a bird of beauty.

She looks like the Queen
Sat on her own in that big wide world.

Leanne Parker (15)
Tarporley Community High School

Leaving Home

I packed my bags and I went,
I packed sandwiches (in case I got hungry),
Sleeping bag (in case I had to sleep outside),
And the cat in his travel box (in case I got lonely).

Now I look back at my expedition,
(Down the street),
And I realised . . .
I was only gone for half an hour.

No wonder when I came back in,
They didn't seem worried
And that annoyed me,
Didn't they care?

You see,
I was only six
And I didn't really have a brain,
I didn't expect to leave them *forever*.

Next week I packed my bags,
The cat, sleeping bag and cake,
But I was going somewhere closer to home,
The cupboard under the stairs.

Alexandra Rollinger (12)
Tarporley Community High School

Night Sky

The dark blue of evening
Mixes with the light blue of day
The clouds combining twisting together
Their colours melt into each other, burning like a fire
Red as a river of blood swirling in deep orange and dull yellow
They seem to stream away from me whisping into nothingness
As I lie there
The sky too early for night and too late for day
The hours between, painting the picture of the day gone by.

William Park (15)
Tarporley Community High School

My Cat

I have a white cat called Thomas
Who is really, really fat
He's twice as fat as an ordinary cat
But he's extremely agile
And uses those furry feet
To jump into the table
And eat Mum's best meat
He sleeps on my bed
And jumps on my head
At seven o'clock in the morning
I see him outside in the field
Clutching his precious yield
Which is usually a rabbit or a mouse
He climbs up our garden tree
And gets stuck on the highest branch you can see
So we have to fetch him down
And we hardly ever frown
As he comes and headbutts my knee!

Robert Cooke (12)
Tarporley Community High School

Monsters

Lurking around corners,
Snarling giants that scurry away,
The unknown blackness,
Terrifying lost souls,
Full of anger,
Gobbling and snacking,
Waiting for the night to come,
Stalking the unlucky few,
Getting ready to pounce,
As fast as the eye can follow.

Nicholas Morrison (13)
Tarporley Community High School

My Dog

My dog, Bailey, has a big black nose
And he really likes to pose.
Bailey is big and yellow,
He is very mellow.
He jumps around all day,
He was born to play.
Bailey likes chasing cats,
He also likes chewing mats.
Bailey is never, ever mean,
He likes football, he is very keen.
Bailey likes chewing flowers,
He could run around for hours and hours.
Bailey likes running round with sticks,
He also likes giving licks.
Bailey has big sharp teeth,
He has them for eating meat.
Bailey has big black paws,
He also has a waggy tail,
He wags it quicker than a snail.

Keris Blaze (12)
Tarporley Community High School

Night-Time

In through the windows, climb the shadows of darkness,
It invades the houses, it fills me with helplessness,
As it crawls through the doorways and up the stairs,
It frightens little children whom it catches unawares,
Out slithers the monster from under the bed,
It moves across the room and fills me with dread,
But all of a sudden, at last comes the new day
And with it comes light, which chases darkness away,
Until the next night, it is locked back where it lay.

Peter Aidley (12)
Tarporley Community High School

Winter Wonderland

Icy breath and rainbow scarves
Woolly mittens and chuttering cars
Welly boots and crunching leaves
Furry jackets and naked trees
Snapping twigs underneath your feet
The animals are collecting food to eat
Whistling wind and blowing gales
Run inside before it hails!
Dripping rain and bright white snow
The kids rush up and off they go!
The shops are filled with presents galore
Here come the children to see the man they adore
Hooray! Hooray! Father Christmas is here!
Look over there, it's his 12 reindeer!
Waiting in queues to sit on his knee
The children's faces are filled with glee
A laugh, a smile and a *ho, ho, ho!*
Now it is time for Santa to go.

Hannah Brownlee (13)
Tarporley Community High School

Kes

She accelerates rapidly towards him
Sweeps in a downward arc,
Carries high into the air.
She turns and stoops,
Ready for her attack.
She stoops faster and harder,
Eyes fixed, beak open.
Swoops, angling her body adjusting her flight
To any slight shift in speed or direction.
Comes in low, then back high,
Hurtles down towards her prey, head first.
She clutches it,
Swoops down to the ground.

Grace Styles (15)
Tarporley Community High School

Revenge Is Sweet

He, he, he,
Let's run away,
Upstairs or downstairs,
Let's hide for a day.

Will Mum find the maggots
Lying in her bed
Or the massive spider
That looks as if it's dead?

It's really her own fault,
She shouldn't have been so mean,
Serves her right, the evil mum,
I wasn't anywhere when she asks me where I've been.

Maybe I went too far with the maggots
And the spider that appears to be dead,
The worms crawling in her soup,
Now I won't get fed.

Yes, I'll go and tell her,
I'll make up by buying her an enormous chocolate bar,
Oh no, it's too late, she's found out now,
I can tell because I heard an
Aaaaaaaarrrrrrgggggghhh!

Meredith Roberts (12)
Tarporley Community High School

I Can't Write Poems

I can't write poems, even if I try
I stare blankly at the ceiling
And imagine it's the sky
Boredom and panic are feelings
Why do people write poetry?
It seems such a waste of time
When we should be outside and free
Who cares about rhythm and rhyme?

Jamie Davies (13)
Tarporley Community High School

The Flight Of A Hawk

A speck appears on the horizon,
Growing closer;
It holds like a star
Then swoops and disappears.

Reappears like a roller coaster,
Up and down;
Lands, standing on the pole,
A god-like figure,
Eyes wide looking for its next victim.

Stop! Takes off;
In search of her next meal,
Heads my way,
Gliding towards me as if she'd known me forever,
What should I do?

Richard Ankers (15)
Tarporley Community High School

My Family

My family is *mad!*
They're always shouting about something
Whether I've done something wrong
Or something good has happened
They're *mad!*
Two dogs, a cat and three horses,
It's the madhouse
Or also known as a zoo!
My bedroom's a pigsty!
Well, it's better than my sister's!
My sister's six
And a complete nutter.
My mum's lost it
And I'm the only sane one!
But I still love them!

Rebecca Ward (13)
Tarporley Community High School

Kes

Silence,
Brown eyes open,
Glass eyes,
Curved beak, ajar,
Life fading.

The hawk flaps her wings,
Fans her tail,
Beautiful brown eyes,
Threaten, piercing, alert,
Then turn, stoop,
Faster, harder,
Flying in a pocket of silence,
Fierce, wild, independent,
Breast heaving,
Standing proud.

A fan-like wing,
A feathered instrument,
Notes too soft,
Life faded,
Silence.

Christine Howard (15)
Tarporley Community High School

Wind And Rain

Have you ever felt the wind
Blowing on your face?
It really feels like a fan
Blowing at full pace.

Have you ever felt the rain
Dripping in your hair?
It makes you feel in all the world
You haven't got a care.

Will Catherall (13)
Tarporley Community High School

The Evacuee

I remember the day I had to say,
Goodbye to my family and friends.
I remember when I packed my bag
And attached to my neck a cardboard tag.

I remember waiting in the rain,
Waiting for that mystery train.
Then down the track came two bright eyes,
Round and welcoming like two apple pies.

The train stopped with an almighty hiss,
As I stepped out the sun shone like bliss.
But then I was put in a line to be picked,
Some of the children screamed and kicked.

I remember the day when I was last,
I remember just wanting to get home fast.
The waiting and watching just me and my pen
And remembering it would never be the same again.

Harriet Mulcahy (13)
Tarporley Community High School

Fear!

The wind whistled, howling at the door,
Do I run away or stay and listen to more?
Rattle, bang, hiss, sigh,
Do I stay or say goodbye?
Like a typhoon swirling around,
Will it continue or go to ground?
I can't decide just what to do,
Floorboards creaking, headache too,
Indecision that's not me, I'm usually good
With all I see,
But at this moment it's pitch-black,
No candles, lights to guide me back,
In a panic, I make a run,
Have decided it's no fun.

Luke Robinson (13)
Tarporley Community High School

The Dress

As I walk in the shop
And see all the clothes,
I look around
And see the one thing I want to own.

As it hangs on the rail,
Looking better than ever,
Its bright pink colours
Makes me want to wear it forever!

I pick it up and look in the mirror,
It makes me feel so much better.
I put it back on the hanger,
Now, I'm sad!

Oh I do wish I could afford it,
As I walk away and leave it there,
It looks so alone,
That beautiful dress

Is not mine to own!

Lucy Phillips (13)
Tarporley Community High School

United

Old Trafford
The reds go marching wide and wide
It's like the ghost train is a ride
Up and down and to and fro
There is no other place to go
The chant of the crowd
It makes me proud
To say I am one of them
One of those who support the men
The 11 players who do their best
They've won the game and all the rest.

Lee Dutton (13)
Tarporley Community High School

Old Trafford 1998

As I enter the stand
I feel like a grain of sand
Compared to the 70 thousand fans
Who raise their hands
For our eleven men
While the other team is on ten
United fans are laughin'
Bayern fans are cryin'
As the final whistle blows
The game comes to a close
Bayern hang their heads low
United fans crow
Don't know why they bother comin'
We always end up winnin'.

Adam Edwards (13)
Tarporley Community High School

War!

Gunfire,
It's still here,
The war is gone,
It's still here,
The pain of fighting,
It's still here.

People died,
They're still here,
Bodies gone,
They're still here,
A new day dawns,
War's still here.

Ruth Hardern (13)
Tarporley Community High School

Test Day

Silence!
Everyone's looking around them,
No one's moving.
People checking they've got their pens,
Which one will they be choosing?
We all walk in the hall,
It reminds me of our school ball,
Everyone sits down,
No one looks around.
Slowly the time ticks by,
Not a sound, not a cry,
Pens swiftly moving all around me,
People far as I can see.
Finally the teachers talk,
We all stand up, begin to walk,
The test is over, we all shout,
We don't know what about.
We all smile as we look back,
We all did it, it's in the sack,
Finally we talk about our friends,
Who weren't there on test day!

Natalie Dean (13)
Tarporley Community High School

It's Your Fault!

We're always moving house!
It makes me feel like a mouse
So small and helpless!
One day in one place
The next in another
It's all because
Of my mother
She's always getting bored
We're like a boat
But never moored.

Melanie Kukla (13)
Tarporley Community High School

The Day I Saw A Witch

One cold autumn night,
When I was camping in the wood,
I heard a cackle and on the moon so bright,
I saw a witch, covered in blood.

I tried to hide but it was too late,
She saw me and swooped to the floor,
She looked at me with a murderous twitch,
What happened next is a blur.

I awoke in chains on a mountain top,
Bones surrounded my feet,
Something was lurking in the shadows,
My heart drumming with a constant beat.

Then she came, the hellion,
I was filled with fear and dread,
'I see you've met my pet, my son,
Fear not for soon you'll be dead.'

From the shadows, the thing it came,
It smelt of death, it stank,
It ripped out my heart and showed it me,
Before it gulped and drank.

A warning to campers afar,
Beware of the full moon you see,
Or the hellion witch will take your soul,
To a hell world just like me!

Martin Hall (14)
Tarporley Community High School

The Beautiful Game

It starts with one,
A man amidst the masses.
He just strikes up a tune,
But it catches on, like a virus.
Louder and louder until soon
It rises to a deafening crescendo
And then, silence, it dies down
And the crowd resumes an eerie silence,
To make way for the echo of the wind.
The players on the pitch are the stars of today,
But the stars of tomorrow are mere miles away . . .

. . . Small boys in the park.
Jumpers for goalposts, running around,
Not a care in the world.
Their young imaginations run wild.
Oh, the sheer bliss of being a child.
But everyone knows they're not young for long,
Soon they'll be the ones who start up the song.

Dominic Gidge (13)
Tarporley Community High School

Waves Of Blue

Come to this massive ground,
The noise is just so loud.
Everton and Leicester too,
As waves of blue
Sing
'Come on you Blues!'
Hoping that we wouldn't lose
The bright, warm sun was out
Suddenly a louder shout
As the final whistle blew
Everybody knew
It was a match we should have won
But it was only a bit of fun!

Simeon Aidley (14)
Tarporley Community High School

A Game Of Chase

A game of chase,
Started off a race,
Darkness draws near
And yet we show no fear.

Rocks and cliffs bigger than I,
I feel like an ant under the sky,
The sky like a black blanket of stars,
Bones everywhere like a graveyard.

The loneliness yet I am not alone,
My loyal dog barking at every noise,
Though he would not let on,
He smelt my fear,
Knowing I wish I was far away from here.

Fenced like an animal in a cage,
Trying to get out though I know, no way,
Cars with headlights that look like eyes,
Coming towards us in the midnight sky.

A shadow drawing near,
A shadow of a beast,
I take a look and see,
Yet it only appears to be,
A small rodent following me.

At last we are found
And homeward-bound,
To find a house full of people,
Just to see whom won the race,
But I'm afraid to say it wasn't me!

Lauri Steel (13)
Tarporley Community High School

Fairies

At the bottom of the garden
Deep underground
There's a wonderful
Magical secret land

Full of little people
With tiny wings
What are these strange
And beautiful things?

They're fairies of course!
To see them's a must
With their faith, trust and . . .
Pixie dust.

Leighanne Proctor (13)
Tarporley Community High School

Battle Of The Elements

Waves crashing
Against the weak ship
Much more than a storm
A mean, whirling tornado
People struggle and scream
Unbalanced by the twisting
Rocking vessel

Just a dot
Right in the middle of a battle
The skies against the sea
And after it all ends
There is just silence
Waiting until once again
The sea rebels.

Ellen Jeffrey (13)
Tarporley Community High School

Miserable

It's wet and cold outside
It's all so miserable
There's no noise
Ever so quiet
What happened to people?
No friends to see
All alone, everyone's inside
As it's pouring down

I might catch a cold outside
You never know
As it's ever so cold
My mother always said
If you didn't put a coat on
You'd catch a cold
I should have listened to my mother
I thought I was big
But at the end of it all
I have (sniff)
A cold!

Lucy Unsworth (13)
Tarporley Community High School

The Moon

There it is so far away
A circle of light shiny and round as a pearl
No man has ever been there but that will soon change
The first man is landing
From here he is as tiny as a dot
We watch on our TV screens as he hops around
The moon like a kangaroo.

Anthony Howard (14)
Tarporley Community High School

Summer Has Gone!

Summer has gone,
Winter is here.
The cold breath air,
Winter is here.
Coats and gloves, hats and scarves,
No adults about but
The cold breath air.
Children playing,
Snow on the ground,
The rain comes down,
Wet on the ground.
Water all around,
Summer has gone,
Winter is here.

Louise Rogers (13)
Tarporley Community High School

Niagara Falls

The immensity of it all
And the noise of the gushing water,
Sends you into great awe.

The air around is full of dampness,
Wet to breathe it in,
The day was hot
But the water kept on coming.

On the boat, 'The Maid of the Mist',
Taking us up to the falls.
We were like tiny, little blue ants
Getting swallowed by the mist.

The noise was intense,
But not loud enough to drown out
The Texan behind screaming,
'We're in the middle of Niagara.'

Christopher Clifford (13)
Tarporley Community High School

A Flight Of Angels

A flight of angels
Landed in my dark
A thousand flakes
Fell from the darkness
Showering me in white
The angel I knew
Appeared before me
Pressing a finger to my lips
Her wings high above
Clothed in pure white
Feathers dove-like
Flakes of frost
She left around me
One blemish in all that purity
Their wings continued
A rhythmic beating
A blinding light in the dark.

Carmela Farrington (13)
Tarporley Community High School

Winter

In the middle of November,
Winter has set in,
Icy frost lies on the ground,
Glistening in the winter sun,
The air is cold,
Mist is around,
The icy wind chops into your face,
Snow starts to fall,
Little kids go out to play,
Christmas is nearly here,
Another end to another year.

Natalie Boulton (13)
Tarporley Community High School

The Wolf

The moon glows bright,
You can hear no sound,
Hunting by moonlight,
The great wolf howls,
Searching for a moment,
Searching for a sight,
This wolf hunts alone
And this wolf hunts by night.
This wolf has no pack,
A lone wolf with no friends.
This wolf hunts for itself,
For itself it fends.
The pine trees sway,
As if on wings,
Deep in the forest,
A wolf howls to the wind.

William Kirkman (13)
Tarporley Community High School

Autumn Fairies

Autumn fairies come out to play,
They sit there in midday,
The trees that surrounded stood upright,
Hiding the secretive fairies
Like a noble groom and bride.
Acorns fall and conkers too
Like small, abandoned fairies' hats
That they may use.
Autumn leaves swirl like a whirlpool
Down on the floor,
Fairies here and fairies there,
Autumn fairies everywhere.

Annabelle Greco (13)
Tarporley Community High School

Thunder And Lightning

With a clap of thunder
And a flash of lightning
I hid my head under the duvet
The lightning blazed like someone
Flicking a light on and off

The thunder drums
Another bang
Something lights up the sky
Lightning
The stars hide behind the clouds
Like they are frightened too
In my bedroom shaking with fear
Another bang
Shaking my wardrobes
Why do I have to be alone?
Bang! I count
1 . . . 2 . . . 3 *bang!*

Kerri Rogers (13)
Tarporley Community High School

Angels

Angels always watching, always out of sight,
Always making sure you're doing the things that are right,
My grandma is an angel, she died a while ago,
She had always taught me the things I ought to know,
Her sweet and gentle smile, her arms are open wide,
Watching over my shoulder and there by my side,
Even when I'm happy or sad,
Even when I'm good or bad,
My grandma's always with me,
I know that she can see,
I have an angel watching over me.

Becki Remelie (13)
Tarporley Community High School

Riding

I like to ride out at weekends
It's really hard to do
It takes me a long time
To get my horse to go

Through the fields we canter
Along the lanes we trot
It's very energetic
And I like it a lot

I spend times at the stables
Giving horses carrots for tea
I go home quite exhausted
It's very good for me.

Richard Smith (13)
Tarporley Community High School

Winter

White blankets cover the earth
Chandeliers of ice hang from branches
As snowflakes fall slowly from the sky
Spinning and twirling around
Icicles like jewels hang from silent buildings
Christmas is coming, yeah
The wind is whistling through the air
Christmas trees glowing like a rainbow.

Michelle Remelie (13)
Tarporley Community High School

Dark Shadows

The dark shadows glide,
Through the star shimmering skies,
I hear the beating like a low drum beat,
As the wings lift and fall.
They notice each other and call,
Landing on a branch the talons piercing the young tree,
He calls again,
His scarlet tongue can be seen,
Inside his orange beak,
They come together,
Black shapes on the skyline,
Crows.

Gabrielle Macpherson (13)
Tarporley Community High School

Weather At Christmas

Snow is like icing sugar falling from the sky,
Like shooting stars flashing by,
I look below,
My feet buried in two inches of snow.

With icicles, dangerous daggers dangling from the roof,
The stars in the sky are shining bright,
The raindrops are bouncing off the ground,
Everybody's in bed and there's no sound.

Jacqui Jones (13)
Tarporley Community High School

One Moment

One moment changes millions of lives
This one moment will send millions into despair
Yet millions into joy
Everyone watching
Everyone listening
Waiting to see what happens
In this one moment
Everyone holding their breath
Everyone silent
Waiting to see what happens
In this one moment
Everyone still
Everyone praying
Waiting to see what happens
When the penalty is taken.

Jack Heaton (15)
Tarporley Community High School

The Panther

The panther strolls the night, silently it gets ready
To pounce quickly and stealthily on the unsuspecting prey,
It poises there,
Unmoving like a coiled spring,
Suddenly *bang* it shoots off like a rocket and lands on its prey,
Its razor-sharp claws tearing at flesh and bone.

Matthew Hardman (13)
Tarporley Community High School

A Place I Once Called Home

In this dull, dark room,
Happy memories glisten like the sun,
But when did the room get dark?
When did the lights dim then die?

In reality,
    Silence!
In my head, crashing thunder,
    My thoughts waiting for lightning to strike again.

        Alone, yet voices,
            Shouting shrilling sounds,
            Voices of the past almost brought back to life.

When did this room get dark?
When will I hear angels whispers lead me to light?
    A place I once called home.

Eve Byrne (15)
Tarporley Community High School

Sunshine

Like a big orange against blue paper,
It glares down on the masses,
Clouds float like sponges on water,
Hot, hot like an oven,
No water around, a drought is occurring,
An ice cream van plays its hypnotising music,
Putting everyone in a trance,
Then the rain comes,
Everyone flees the picturesque scene,
Like running from death.

Hannah Fraser-Smith (15)
Tarporley Community High School

Changing World

I'm curled up in a hiding place,
Like a caterpillar inside its case.
I'm hiding from that changing place,
Where there's pollution here, there, underground and in the air,
Shall I stay or shall I go?
This world is all that I know!
Safe and content in all that I do.

I respect our world, wherever I go,
I leave nothing but footsteps and take nothing but memories.

Do they think the rubbish has legs?
What! As if it's going to jump into the bin itself,
The world's a ticking bomb,
Its days are limited,
Help it now and it could live on!

Julian Eldridge (13)
Tarporley Community High School

The Hunter

The hunter sits in wait,
Silent,
He doesn't twitch, he doesn't move,
Just waits.
His traps are set; his gun is loaded
And his family are hungry,
He's not a murderer or animal,
He's just a poacher.
He takes what he needs
And leaves what he doesn't,
Nothing goes to waste.

Martin Lee Chrimes (13)
Tarporley Community High School

Autumn

The leaves are changing
Into golden coins falling
From the tree

      Marigolds tangled bright
      And bold, blazing orange
      And gold.

Conkers scattered around
The trees, in amongst the
Fallen leaves.

      The warmth of summer
      Has grown old and now
      Has left us with brown
      And gold.

Amy Struthers (13)
Tarporley Community High School

An Icy Winter

Days have got darker,
Temperatures colder,
Snow swirls round like dancing fairies,
Icicles hang below my window,
Pointing dangerously like daggers ready to pierce its victim,
Frosted leaves are left upon the glowing white trees,
Glistening in the sunlight,
Milky-coloured clouds drift slowly overhead,
As a cool breeze whistles through the amazing white wilderness.

Katie Enwright (13)
Tarporley Community High School

The Mountains Of Glory

Far in the distance you may see
The mountains, dominant in all their splendour,
Covered in trees that sing to the sun.

The lakes so deep, you can't see the bottom
And the whine of the whales,
Like the sound of a mourning mother.

The glacier, a river of ice,
Hanging between the ancient peaks,
Never to flow again

And the wolves howl,
As the moon watches over
Nature in all its glory.

Ben Rogers (13)
Tarporley Community High School

The Left Winger

There goes the little number eleven
Bamboozling opponents with his
Silky skills and dazzling dribbling

Twisting and turning in and out
He hugged the touchline
While he sped past defenders
Doing cheeky nutmegs and classy step-overs

He left four defenders in his wake
He fooled another with a double shuffle
From his rapid dancing feet.

Christopher Jones (13)
Tarporley Community High School

A Winter Wonderland

The days get darker,
Though the sky is bright.
A crisp, softened footprint,
Sinks into the white.

Trees are no longer,
A glowing green.
White is all that
Surrounds the scene.

Our town is lit up,
By these pearls
And gathered in the street
Are boys and girls.

Hats and scarves,
Whistle through the air.
Snowballs are made,
Entwined with care.

Frost starts to turn,
Slowly to brown.
Slush begins to
Cover the ground.

Now it's gone
And spring is near.
Winter comes but
Once a year.

Emma Corbett (13)
Tarporley Community High School

Getting Up

Getting up for school, it really is a bother,
Getting shouted at by my rude idle father.
Pulling off the covers, walking down the stairs,
Thinking what to do when my eyes begin to glare.
Someone's burnt my pancakes and there's no gel for my hair.

Richard Howells (11)
Tarporley Community High School

Prison

What is prison?
Family is prison,
Carrots on Monday,
Pie on Tuesday,
Night, doors are locked into the mind,
No inspiration left.

What is prison?
School is prison,
Padlocked thoughts out of reach,
Around the corner,
Time ticks on,
Second, minute, hour, forever
Home, school, home.

What is prison?
Society is prison,
It consumes us,
Slowly eats at our free will,
Until death calls!

What is prison?
The world is prison,
The system holds us back,
Binds us down,
No one is free,
Everyone is trapped.

Samuel George (11)
Tarporley Community High School

Summer Day

Flowers blooming everywhere,
So many that everyone can share,
The sun is shining in the sky,
Now autumn comes passing by.

Becky Jones (11)
Tarporley Community High School

A Breath

A breath,
A single displacement,
Taking time.

The effort,
The reaching grasp,
Trying to take your life.

Stationary,
Your pain,
Finding no end,
Drags you down.

You find, you reach,
The end.

Peter Kirby (11)
Tarporley Community High School

Football

The tension's rising,
The sweat dripping down
His forehead,
Anelka places the ball
On the spot.
He steps up,
Howard's flying through
The air.
He holds his head
In despair.
He scores the penalty,
That puts them top,
Leaving United behind.

Joel Robinson (11)
Tarporley Community High School

Shhh

Shhh
Everything's quiet,
Everything's silent,
It's the night before Christmas Day.

Shhh
Wide awake, my eyes glaring
Into space, my eyes staring.

Shhh
Can I hear him coming?
Christmas carols he is humming.

Shhh
Hear the presents he is bringing,
Now I can hear him leaving.

Shhh
Up the chimney onto the roof,
People said Santa did not exist
But now I know the truth.

Shhh
I hear him glide away on his sleigh.

Shhh
Now I'll go to sleep
All the way to *Christmas Day!*

Laura Pattinson (11)
Tarporley Community High School

Autumn

A utumn days are coming,
U nder a moonlit sky,
T he trees are turning brown,
U mbrellas are out, leaves fly,
M y favourite season, wild and fresh,
N ow winter comes, I say goodbye.

Emma Bruce (11)
Tarporley Community High School

My Poem

Birds sing
And fly around,
Bees sting
And buzz around.
Butterflies flutter
And float in the wind.
Horses trot
And often walk.
Parrots screech
And sometimes talk.
Frogs ribbit
And like to hop.
Squirrels run
Before they stop.
Last of all
The spiders that crawl.

Sarah Bowyer (12)
Tarporley Community High School

My First Day Of School

The uniform is bland,
The writing hurts my hand.
The classes are so boring,
The pupils can't help snoring.
The sandwiches are great,
The doughnuts I really hate.
The PE lesson rushes past,
The maths lesson, isn't fast.
Now it is the end of the day,
I can't wait to get away.

Adam Hayward (11)
Tarporley Community High School

Over The Ocean!

Over the ocean,
Fish swimming,
Dolphins diving,
Birds colliding.

Boat sailing,
People waving,
Sea churning,
Waves soaring,
As we go by.

We're getting closer,
Figures emerging,
Places reoccurring,
Boat shaking,
Sun straining,
Suddenly stopping.

Molly Owen (11)
Tarporley Community High School

The Horizon

I gently rise from under the ground, up and above the clouds.
I'm here all day, for the children play, out and about,
I bring light to the world, instead of you being dark and dull.
I move from place to place every single minute of the day.
Early mornings, I start to rise while you're all asleep,
Late at night I start to set, while you're all indoors.
I'm down for 12 hours, then I wake up, then I'm up all day.
When I set, everything changes shape and size
And it all looks black and dull.

Jessica Noyes (11)
Tarporley Community High School

Dolphins

Dolphins swimming about in water
Splashing about
Having fun
Dolphins

Dolphins searching for fish
In order to eat
She's hungry now
Dolphins

Dolphins, she's swimming about
Now she's full
It's the end of one long day
Dolphins.

Laura Williams (12)
Tarporley Community High School

A Chocolate Orange

Silky smooth centre
Tantalising my taste buds
Luxurious pleasure
Stomach curling up
Like a sleek cat, consuming its own delicious sleep
Savouring the last few scraps
It's over
No more
Gone.

Jamie Johnstone (11)
Tarporley Community High School

Dust Devils

I have read of dust devils
That silently whisper across
The silvery-white sands of the desert
To play on the horizon
And sway like drunks across the valleys
As then in the distance storm clouds gather
And a few drops fall, leaving dark tears
In the dusty earth, but not enough
To deter the dust devils from dancing
Like mirages across the plain
Taunting as if to say 'we fooled you'
Then those miniature cyclones swirl away
Like ghosts rising out of the ground
As it rains only dust
All colour from the sunset, a thick dusty red
Is bled from the sky as night falls
The tumbleweeds in great stampedes
Are tossed and blown, as dust devils slowly rise
And whistling and whirling reach for the sky
With fingers outstretched as if begging for grace
It will be hot and dry again tomorrow
These whirling dervishes bring on the night
As they scavenge the ground with their tentacles
Snatching and devouring anything in their path
And then, suddenly, their hectic form is lost
Scattered by the night winds across the desert
The last dust devil swirls past and soon is out of sight.

Tarryn Peinke (14)
Tarporley Community High School

Forever Friends

Children screaming,
Children fighting,
Children punching,
Children biting.
Not happy with each other,
Some are hiding undercover,
In the end, always friends again,
They've made up, the time has come,
Forever friends with everyone!

Lydia McDougall (11)
Tarporley Community High School

Anger

The vicious volcanoes stood peacefully,
Until I had the feeling in my heart.

The volcanoes were bubbling,
Bombs were exploding
And the sun was burning bright.

Devils darted from Hell,
Memories of hatred were swirling at the back of my brain.

My blood was like a pile of sizzling sausages,
Although the sky's turned scarlet the thoughts flew to Hell.

I felt the slime of the underworld,
The screams of the souls trapped under.

Suddenly I imagined a quick vision of the underworld,
Fires were powered by the souls of evil.

Lava was erupting,
But souls were being tortured by devils.

As sour as a lemon is *anger*,
But never as sweet as a melon.

Hassan Kamran (11)
The King's School in Macclesfield

Anger Is . . .

Anger swells up in me like a flame in my stomach,
It makes me all hot and sweaty,
My blood runs hot and sometimes cold,
Like lava in a volcano.

It feels like ragged rocks and sharp glass
And tastes like sour lemons,
The devil within me just wants to break free,
Like a flash of lighting in the dark.

A volcano in me just wants to erupt
And spurt out my deepest feelings,
But I keep them locked up inside,
Knowing that one day they will come back and haunt me.

William Allen (11)
The King's School in Macclesfield

Anger

Anger is a picture, a picture of your other side,
It shows your Devil who is living in Hell,
The Devil records your anger,
Whether as fierce as a volcano,
Or as harmless as a fly,
Your anger tastes bitter,
When you listen you hear,
Crime, gunshots, people crying out,
You have to tell your anger,
Or the Devil will have you,
Then your anger will create *fear*.

Alex Smith (11)
The King's School in Macclesfield

Anger

Anger swelled up as if it was a devil inside me
It is like an earthquake breaking friendships up
It's like a wave wiping a friendship out
It crumbles you
Makes you feel blood hot
It's like an uncontrollable fire which burns everything in its path

When hurtful things are often said
What do you gain?
When you've lost your temper
And you've said things you don't mean
You feel sad about what you've said.

Edward Morris (11)
The King's School in Macclesfield

A Bad Dream

I thought I saw my friend fade away
And I found myself drowning in the tumbling billows of the main
I saw dead men's skulls with jewels like eyes
And thousands of men that fishes gnawed upon
I thought what pain it was to drown
And what dreadful noise of water in mine ears
I saw my own death within my eyes
How horrible it would be, drowning in this horrible place
Reflecting jewels on the seabed
So shiny it hurt mine eyes to see.

Ben Monro (11)
The King's School in Macclesfield

Anger

I slump down in the chair,
Head bent and held in hands.
Silence saturates the room.
Lips feel dry, mouth tastes bitter,
The smell of betrayal sickens me.
Questions thump inside my mind:
Why did he? How could he? Let me down?
My body feels fragile and empty.
Anger starts to feed my weakness,
Pumping strength through my veins.
Teeth clench in defence, fists tighten to attack,
Beads of sweat glisten on my brow.
Words fire from my mouth like bullets.
He is as cold as a statue
And shows no flicker of remorse.
Drained from all my anger,
I walk away alone.

Jamie Butterworth (11)
The King's School in Macclesfield

Anger Poem

Anger can grow slowly, like a tiny seed.
It can grow quickly to be a mighty flame.

Anger can be terrible, like a volcano erupting.
It can be short but sharp like a lighting bolt.

Anger can be bitter, like a sour lemon.
It can be sweet like soft, deceitful smiles.

Anger can be anything, if you keep it in,
But if you let it out, it will pass like the wind.

Thomas Waters (12)
The King's School in Macclesfield

Anger

My mouth was dry,
I was boiling over,
I could smell my sweat.
The Earth was quaking:
It sounded like a turbo
Charged car revving up.

My friend looked as if he
Had just bitten a hot chilli.
Flames and smoke were
Coming out of his ears.
He looked as if he was going to blow.

We were lightning-quick
On replying to each other.
We felt as if sharp knives were dug into us,
We were like sour lemons.

We needed to be refreshed,
By a big wave rushing over us.
Then we would be friends again.

Daniel Cotterill (11)
The King's School in Macclesfield

Anger

Anger swelled up like a volcano erupting
I saw a giant bolt of lightning smash across the sky
I could taste hate and deceit
My patience was burning faster than the fuse on dynamite
My insides were burning with hate
A rocket taking off inside me
I was snatched away by pure hate.

Krishnan Rathod (12)
The King's School in Macclesfield

My Anger

To me he was the Devil,
Anger, hatred and death.
His eyes were like fire,
Burning into mine.

Constantly he beat me,
He used a steel-tipped whip.
Day and night I lived in fear,
While my anger continued to boil.

Then one night I took a knife
And while he lay asleep,
I stole into his bed chamber
And at last I got my revenge.

Satisfied, my work was done,
I left the house at dawn.
I walked out of the gates, straight out of Hell
And went on the road to Heaven.

Adam Cummings (11)
The King's School in Macclesfield

Anger Poem

Anger's like a volcano
Waiting to erupt
It starts off calm
Then gets wild
When it's going to blow up

The burning smell
Can make you sick
The evil sight
Can hurt

The touch of it
Burns to your heart
The taste of it's
Like dirt.

Henry Jeffrey (11)
The King's School in Macclesfield

Anger

Anger is like a tornado,
Ripping through the sky, battering all the houses.
Anger is like a lightning bolt,
Tearing through the sky,
Killing useless humans and pets.
Anger is like an earthquake,
Shaking houses to the ground.
When you're angry, you feel blood in your mouth,
You feel like a piece of dynamite about to explode.
You think you are the Devil.
You storm out through the door
With horns sticking out through your head,
Ready to poke someone.
You see a sharp rock coming down on top of your head,
You see some hot lava coming down the volcano,
Going to kill the person who angered you. Then, he is dead.

Nicholas Wrigley (11)
The King's School in Macclesfield

Anger Poem

The Devil was taking over my body,
The brewing of the lava started to burn,
My volcano exploded,
The lava was spilling rapidly,
An earthquake broke out,
My hate growing,
I tasted blood in my mouth,
My kettle was boiling,
I felt like a sharp knife was cutting me,
I felt like dynamite exploding in a mine shaft,
A T-rex was roaring in my head,
I saw him,
I saw him,
I saw the Devil!

Guy Hopkinson (11)
The King's School in Macclesfield

Anger

A burning flame comes inside me,
A dynamite burning heart,
Anger is pulsating all the way through me,
Like a strong and roaring wind.

The anger is like lightning coming from the sky,
It is like a great white shark biting into me,
Sweat dripping down my face,
Like a sour lemon.

Steam coming out my ears,
Flowing around my face,
A thousand hot chillis in my mouth
And the Devil's dirty face.

Earthquakes trembling everywhere now,
All over my body,
Red-hot fury all about,
Still keeps on growing.

Ciaran Hanrahan (11)
The King's School in Macclesfield

Anger

Anger is a flame, burning up the brain,
A flash of lightning through the head,
That makes it so you can't sleep in bed,
An atomic bomb going off in a drain,
Dynamite shattering the windowpane,
It tastes like hot chilli,
It tastes like sour milk,
It smells like rotten eggs,
It feels like sharp knives,
The Devil thrashing in my rib cage,
Trying to break free,
I feel like a bull, I'm seeing red
And I'm now about to charge.

Anthony Boden (11)
The King's School in Macclesfield

Anger Poem

Anger swelled up in me
Like a volcano about to erupt

My temper grew shorter
Like a fuse on a bomb

My anger started to grow
Like the cracks in the ground in an earthquake

I felt like an avalanche roaring down a mountain
My enemy felt like a tree in my path of destruction

Anger burnt inside me
A ball of fire waiting to be released

Flashes of aggression struck
Like bolts of lightning appearing out of the darkness of my mind

My anger rose sharply
As though it were being dragged upwards by a spinning tornado.

Ben Holden (11)
The King's School in Macclesfield

An Endless Battle . . .

The battle of the sea and shore rages
The waves thrash against the land.
Slowly reshaping and changing landscapes,
The white foam engulfs the sand.

Rain pours down and lightning crackles in the storm
The skies are dark and full of clouds
The scene could send chills down your spine
In the background, thunder rumbles aloud.

Even though the battle is far from over
The storm clouds slowly say goodbye.
The waves reluctantly calm down
And the sun appears once more in the sky.

The sea becomes friendly once again
It turns into a bright and sunny day.
Who would have known that truce would be declared
Between the land and sea in such an unexpected way?

The day goes by uneventfully
Soon it is time for the sun to say goodbye
As it gradually disappears beyond the horizon
All the colours of the rainbow flood the sky.

The scene fills spectators with awe
Such a beautiful sight is rarely seen.
Enjoy the serenity before the truce is over,
And the battle begins once more between the land and the sea . . .

Kriti Upadhyay (14)
The Queen's School

The Oily Puddle

A fallen rainbow at my feet
A blackened rippling silky sheet
A dead crow, sprawled on the ground
A shining spiral going round and round

A waterfall gushing
A river rushing
Drip and dropping
Never stopping

A sticky sleek coat
Like water rippling beside a boat

It smells of a garage very old
A new car shining like gold.

Lorna Jones (11)
Upton High School

The Cauliflower

Like an unused brain,
Tiny pieces of crisp popcorn,
With long green leaves like arms

And a sound of complete stillness,
But drop it and it's
Like a thudding of giant boots.

A feeling of hard, old concrete,
A stale cookie with chocolate chips on top,
Like bare, rocky Earth.

Sarah Clare (12)
Upton High School

The Sunflower

As bright as a hot summer's day
It is as beautiful as the golden sunshine
Like a yellow daffodil reaching towards the sun
As colourful as a beautiful rainbow

As sticky as candyfloss on a day at the fair
It's as delicate as a newborn baby
Hairy like a rabbit freshly born
Spiky like a thorn bush

It smells like a fresh spring day
It's like a whole field of flowers dancing in the gentle breeze
Like animals in the woodland on a calm day

It sounds like crunchy leaves swirling
And twirling like a ballerina
Like a crackling firework shooting in the night's sky
And blossoming into a marvellous sight.

Michelle Newell (12)
Upton High School

Shell

It looks like the top of an acorn
And half of the horn of a unicorn.

It feels like smooth wax
And a baby after a soothing bath.

It smells like perfume
And some soap with a mild fume.

It sounds like a waterfall falling
And the calm ocean calling.

Jerri Lightfoot (11)
Upton High School

The Shell

What am I?
I look like a dark cave
Welcoming the evil
I look like a small egg
Just about ready to hatch
I look like a big wet mouth
Waiting to eat its prey!

What am I?
I feel like a new sharp razor
Smooth on the top
But sharp on the bottom

What am I?
I smell like the seabed
With fish swimming up and down.

What am I?
I sound like the wind
And waves crushing on the rocks

I look like a dark cave
I feel like a razor
I smell like the sea
I sound like the wind
What am I?

I'm a shell.

Thomas Hostick (11)
Upton High School

The Shell

Like a cave, it doesn't show its insides,
A mouth with razor teeth,
Like an egg, round and smooth.

Listen and it sounds like the ocean waves,
It's like the wind, whistling in the trees.

It is smooth and even,
But then it feels razor-sharp like spikes,
Round like a ball.

A smell of the seaside,
Like the shore and the sand,
The smell of where it once lived.

Josh Carvel (11)
Upton High School

The Sunflower

The sun on a leafy stem,
A fiery flame burning.
The sun rising up on the land,
Like a yellow rose.

The stem as hairy as spider's legs,
A rough snake with crusty tongues
And petals as dry as crêpe paper.

The sweet smell of a fresh meadow,
In early autumn days,
Like a pile of spicy herbs.

The sound of rain falling
And the crackling, rustling leaves.

Millie Green & Bethany Ronald (11)
Upton High School

A Poem About Poems

Why are poems so difficult to write?
You can spend hours thinking of an idea,
But you still can't think of anything!
You have ideas about flying eagles
Soaring majestically through the air
Or empty houses where the doors creak at night
And the windows howl in the dark.

Then not only do you have to think of an idea,
But you have to put in alliteration and similes,
It's like trying to turn turnips into triangular truffles,
It's not humanly possible!
And also what is this personification?
Where houses are awake and grass whispers in the night,
If such things exist I would like to see or hear them.

Why are poems so difficult to finish?
If you successfully use an idea and put in poetic techniques
You still have to finish the thing!
You can finish it with a joke or a summary,
But worst to finish with is the ancient rhyming couplet,
For it I wish to finish with a rhyme,
I have to waste so much of my time!

Adam Burrell (16)
Upton High School

I'm Not Who I Thought You Were

The scars you left here you can't see,
So you don't know they're hurting me.
The cuts run deep without a trace,
The answer's written on my face.
I still need you, you don't care,
No one said, that love was fair.

Caroline Coxhead (15)
Upton High School

What Is Happening?

The phone rings, a worried
Voice speaks
What is happening?
Nobody tells me,
Another phone call,
Another worried voice,
What is happening?

Sitting silently, waiting,
Still I ask myself,
What is happening?
People rushing, grabbing coats,
Grabbing keys,
What is happening?

A knock at the door,
Into the car,
Still the same question,
In my head,
What is happening?

A flash of blue lights, as
Someone gets out,
Off we go again,
What is happening?

A next day comes,
Sitting at the table,
The silence is broken,
A tear falls, now I
Know what has happened!

Leanne Reynolds (15)
Upton High School

Somewhere, Some Child

I wake up, ready for another day,
I open my curtains and look out.
But somewhere, some child wakes up, all alone
And won't open the splintered shutters,
Because they are scared at what they might see.

I make my way downstairs, greeted by my mum
And I eat my breakfast,
But somewhere, some child stumbles downstairs,
No one there to greet them,
No food to eat.

I rush out of the door,
I'm hoping I will make the bus in time,
But somewhere, some child is hoping,
Hoping there will be a bus.

I sit on the bus
And I talk to my friends,
But somewhere, some child
Sits in silence.

I make my way home,
I argue with my brother and retreat to my room,
But somewhere, some child gets home
And looks at photographs of the family
She used to have.

Holly Power (15)
Upton High School

The Beauty Of War

I'm in a land of beauty,
The sky's a multicoloured wonder,
The birds sing a magnificent chorus,
The floor a carpet of luscious green,
Surrounded by vibrant pinks,
Fiery oranges
And dark reds,
Dark reds.
The red spreads from my feet,
Staining the floor,
Now everything starts to fade away,
All is black,
All is black, the colour is gone.

Mark Walmsley (15)
Upton High School

Women And Farm Pickups

You find yourself grinding through the lanes
In that trusty old faithful, the farm pickup
Despite your repeated attempts at thrashing the engine
It refuses to die
Instead it prefers to watch you suffer
You get to grips with the mighty gear stick
And stiff clutch that gives you nothing but grief
Why is it that it goes like a dream for everyone else
But you?
Even the most sensible shoes make no difference.

Rebecca Jones (15)
Upton High School

A Little Boy Bold

There was once a little boy bold,
Who never did as he was told,
His mother said once
'You're a little ponce'
And he was chucked out into the cold!

Once this little boy was out,
He saw a lady with a snout,
He laughed out in glee,
And shouted, 'Hee, hee'
And said, 'Look at that pig with a pout!'

The lady roared and turned around
And made a stressy sound,
She hit with her purse,
As she decided to curse
And out fell one single pound.

The boy ran away,
As he was to pay,
The old landlord for a flat,
He spoke as he sat,
'Don't waste my time, be on your way.'

There once was a little boy bold,
Who never did as he was told,
He got beaten and battered
And left bruised and tattered,
Because he was chucked out into the cold.

Natasha Andrews (13)
Upton High School

Where Is The Love?

The sky is blue
And I'm lonely,
As it's all true
When they all say,
That I'll have to pay,
I'm just lying on the floor
And the second toringly,
Slamming my dim head on the floor.

The rain is clear,
But I'm mournful,
All that's here,
Only be my grave
And when in my rave,
I'll knock you out of Hell,
I'll be looking beautiful,
You'll never be able to tell.

The water is calm,
I'm ground on low,
You are the harm,
I've been all kind,
So stay out my mind,
Will be hiding in caves,
Till my time is over so,
Just listen to my crashing waves.

The love is pure,
I need your love,
Take heart, be sure,
I'll be imparted,
Come into my world,
Question: where is the love?

Aklima Hay (13)
Upton High School

The Girl Who Haunts Me

It might have been years ago
But it still haunts me
It was such a happy day
Playing with my friends
When suddenly it all stops
The world stops
And time stands still
She's behind me
I feel her breath, it makes my hairs stand on end
She calls me horrible things
But I don't cry
She pushes to the hard, cold floor
She walks away
A horrible smirk on her face
The world starts
And time begins again
But her face still haunts me
And her breath
Still taunts me
Her words stab me like knives
The girl who still haunts
And taunts my dreams.

Robyn Piercy (14)
Upton High School

Time To Query

Have you ever taken a moment to think,
Who decided to call that colour pink?
This is where I begin to query
The biggest brain teasers and oldest theories
Most these answers we'll never know
That doesn't stop us asking though!

This first one's for those who like animals
But I'm sure you'll agree, it was made up by fools
Why is rabbiting named after a silent creature?
No one will know, not even your teacher
Is there really life on Mars?
Will we ever have hover cars?
Here's the daddy, the king, the queen bee!
It's the chicken or the egg you see!
Or . . . is it the egg or the chicken?
No one knows, the clock's still ticking.

Now for those puzzling threats
The ones from your mum that everyone gets
If you're sitting on a high wall
And your mum's afraid you might fall
The worst thing she can say
The most confusing thing you'll hear that day
'If you fall and break your legs, don't come running to me'
Please, if anyone understands that, feel free.

I've decided this is a good place to end
Before I drive you round the bend
I won't get started on Cockney rhyming slang
Or if the universe really is down to the big bang
Half the world's mysteries, I've not even covered
And there are many more yet to be discovered.

Sarah Garwood (15)
Upton High School

My Thoughts To Myself

I'm cruising quietly in the dead of day,
My thoughts to myself,
I look around to see clouds, clouds and more clouds,
I cruise a while longer
And then burst into the light,
I sit and admire the view,
The sea, the land, the sky,
I cruise a while longer,
My thoughts to myself,
Suddenly my world erupts with noise,
I break left, then right, then left again,
All I hear is 'Taka Taka Taka'
And the frantic screams of my friends
As they plunge towards the channel,
Then everything turns white
And I'm cruising quietly in the dead of day,
My thoughts to myself.

Sean Gresty (15)
Upton High School

Dreams

Dreams
Night-time sleep
They enter your head
Full of fantastic emotion
Woken by
Nightmares, spooky, freaky
Dark and cold
Sees the clock 02.20
Rain beating down
Wind howling
Before getting back to sleep
The dream remains . . .
Dreams.

Tim Peers (13)
Upton High School

The Fly

Nobody likes me,
I don't know why.

Is it because
I'm a horrible fly?

I come in many different suits,
Like crane, black, house and fruit.

I buzz through a field
And over a gate.

In through a window
And land on a plate.

A feast of all my favourite tuck,
Potatoes, peas, carrots and duck.

My germs can cause many a sickness,
Malaria, cholera and elephantiasis.

Quite complex I am, although very small,
But really content to just sit on a wall.

I have to watch out for birds, frogs and voles,
As they would just swallow me whole.

Droning around the eggs I've just laid,
A man comes along with a tin of 'Raid'.

He fails to spray me, he's angry and hot,
But here comes his wife and . . . oh no,
Swat!

Matt White (13)
Upton High School

Now She Is Gone

Cancer, cancer, cancer
A horrible thing to have
Treatment does not always come at the right time
My nan she had it in her hand
I always thought she'd be mine

I was only little, I didn't understand
I didn't know the reason why she left my side
It spread around her body
She got weaker by the moment

I saw her at her bed, I lay upon her lap
I waved goodbye but don't know why she left me

Where was she going? I didn't understand
I didn't know the reason why she left my side?

Sarah Dove (13)
Upton High School

The Substitute Teacher

It's the way she looked down,
Down on me,
With her big onion eyes,
Eyes round and pale.

It's the way she asked me,
Asked me, 'Are you OK?'
With her flaring nostrils,
Nostrils that hadn't seen a hanky.

Then suddenly she comes,
Comes over to me,
I think I'm in trouble,
I'm shocked,
She tells me the answer.

Lucy Newell (12)
Upton High School

Work, Work, Work!

Do your homework,
Eat your greens,
Make your bed,
My mum screams.

I don't know why grown-ups do that,
They think we're their personal slaves,
All the work they make us do,
Will lead us to an early grave.

They make us do the nasty jobs,
Like clean the bath or loo,
You know one day, out of spite,
We should fake we have the flu.

They'd kick up a song and dance,
They'd say it isn't fair,
But just to see them clean the dirt,
I really couldn't care.

It'd be great to see them work
And work their fingers to the bone,
But later if I was better,
I'd help them do some jobs (groan).

Chelsea Jones (12)
Upton High School

Looking Out The Windowpane

When I'm travelling on a plane,
Looking through the windowpane,
Clouds pass ever so slowly,
Like fluffy bits of cotton wool
Floating across the sky,
Here and there, no cloud is there,
Sometimes scenes of civilisation appear,
Lights buildings and sometimes fields,
Sometimes even smoke,
That looks like creepy hands gliding
Toward the sky,
On other occasions though,
Vast amounts of luscious water
And here and there the odd boat appears,
Sailing towards the sunlit horizon,
When I'm travelling on a plane,
Looking through the windowpane.

Laura Bennett (13)
Upton High School

The Shark

Waves crash on the sand,
Playing with children,
Everyone's happy.

A sudden scream of fright,
Turning happiness to fear,
Swimming away as fast as they can,
A young child screams.

But not everybody gets away so quick,
The only thing left in the sea is blood,
Floating near the shore.

The king of the sea has fed.

Chloë Jordan (12)
Upton High School

Dreams

I feel kind of stupid
When I lay in bed at night
I wanna live my dreams
But you're always pulling me out

The daylight isn't kind
Open my eyes, I'm blind
I'd rather be in bed
Living in my head

I enjoy being what I am
But I hate what I am
I'll never get anywhere in life
But in my dream I can

I know that I'm safe
I can't be harmed
When I am fast asleep
With lonely thoughts I keep.

Mark Paget (16)
Upton High School

The Bull

There was once a lady from Hull,
Who tried to swallow a bull,
She sharpened her teeth,
Thought he tasted of beef,
Then the lady from Hull became full.

Leigh Calvert (13)
Upton High School

The School Bully

She waits by the lockers,
Does the school bully.
Surrounded by her gang,
Ready to take my money.

I wander down there on my own,
There's something strange, am I alone?
Out of the shadows come three or four,
I make a dash for the nearest door.

They catch me and push me
And poke me and punch,
It ends in a black eye
And no money for lunch.

Several years later and I've got a degree
And this makes me, much better than she.
She works in MacDonald's with a face full of spots,
I'm happily married with a couple of tots.

Sinéad Dempsey (12)
Upton High School

Departure

As he left to do his duty,
Eyes glanced back:
Suburban beauty,
A war to fight but will it pass
But then again long may it last,
Things now past run through his mind,
His only world he leaves behind,
Smothered in dreams,
Defeat or glory?
Marching on to build a story,
Please apologise profusely,
For leaving me to do your duty.

Alexandra Freckleton (13)
Upton High School

The Fly In The Soup

Everyone knows about the fly in the soup
The pip in the pie
The money in the pudding
The porridge too hot, the porridge too cold
The food can never be right
But worst of all is the hair in the sandwich

The maggot in the munchies
Mites in the bread
Chick beak in my friend egg
Spider in the salad
The food can never be right
But worst of all is the ant in the salt

The slug in the lettuce
The cockroach in the cream
The mouse in the cake
The rat in the chocolate
The food can never be right
But worst of all is half of something.

Laura Babbs (15)
Upton High School

Football Matches

I don't remember it very well cos I was only one,
But I remember the first time I was mascot.
I got to go on the pitch, I got a little bit scared.

But 13 years later I remember every match,
The smiles as people find out we are in the play-offs.
But I also remember the disappointments of getting knocked out.

I also remember those few weeks of picketing,
Doing well in pre-season friendlies.
Supporters singing all the Chester chants.

The worst memory was being relegated from division three.
But the best vision is getting back up to the third division.

Lauren Andrews (13)
Upton High School

Please Tell Me

As I sit on my bed,
I wonder who I am,
Am I the one who everyone likes
Or am I the one they dread?
Please tell me!

Am I the one who will be famous?
Am I the one they won't know?
Will my dreams come true
Or will they fade away?
Please tell me!

Will I be the one who's bullied
Or will I be the bully myself?
Will I ever get married
Or will I get left on the shelf?
Please tell me!

But maybe one day
I will find my way through the obstacles,
Maybe my life will turn out alright,
Maybe the jigsaw will become complete,
Please tell me!

Sarah Jenkins (12)
Upton High School

The Trenches

Day and night the bullets fly,
Day and night the people die;
Living in this muddy hole,
Both disease and bullets take their toll.
The never-ending scream and cheer,
Who can tell when the end is near?
Daily we fight through smoke and fire -
Daily we die in this hell of barbed wire.

Christopher Parr (14)
Upton High School

Seasons

Green hills as far as the eye can see,
Streams joining into rivers and move to the ocean.
Fields buzzing with life of flowers and bees,
Trees sway and move with the wind in motion.

Mountainous peaks and snow-capped hills,
Tower on a skyline in the distance.
Then a breeze sweeping the landscape with a chill,
Grasses rustle and jump, as if in a dance.

The snow covers the land in a carpet of white,
Undisturbed, untouched is what is
Visible by birds in flight.
Before it melts away, back into the Earth.

Then it is light once more
And the flowers return,
In the first of which there is only four,
The seasons that is, that constantly tour.

Natalie Wilson (13)
Upton High School

Imagine

Imagine life if everyone was the same,
The same face, a different name.
If everyone had the same colour skin,
If nobody was fat and everybody thin.

Imagine if everyone dressed the same,
If nobody was crippled, retarded or lame.
Imagine if every woman loved the same man,
To imagine this I'll do all that I can.

Because I don't think the world would be an exciting place,
If everyone in it had the same face.
The same colour skin and the same eyes,
Being different is cool, I won't tell lies.

Dionne Pryce (13)
Upton High School

Nightmares

Mind dissolving, vision swimming,
Mist dancing and twirling in your eyes.
Shapes spinning, figures looming,
The real world slipping away.

Faces staring, voices creaking,
The night-time world comes out to play.
Arms reaching, legs kicking,
Snatches of people turn away.

Tossing, turning, colours blending,
Darkness surrounding, light dimming.
Cold sweat moistens the pillow,
Screaming, yelling, shouting, punching,
Gone.

Anna Blain (13)
Upton High School

Private James

It was in the trenches in 1914,
Where Private James was based,
During the black of night,
Was where the young soldier met his fate.

His duty was night watchman,
With two other troops as well,
But it was his habit of cigarettes,
Which proved to be his death knell.

He took a match to a cigarette,
For each of the troop of three,
The first caught an enemy sniper's eyes,
For it was such an easy sign to read,
On the second the sniper took aim,
As he lit the last, the crackles of gunfire came
And poor Private James was slain.

Ben Rigby (13)
Upton High School

First Day At School

I walked to the bus stop,
The bus was already there.
I got on; the older pupils staring,
I sat down next to a girl,
I didn't say a word.

The bus soon stopped outside a huge school,
I walked to the hall with my friends.
Teachers introduced themselves.
I listened carefully though I knew I couldn't remember them.

They called out forms and sixth formers took us to our form rooms.
We sat down at a desk and had to introduce ourselves.
The bell soon rang,
Our form tutor walked us to our English room.

I sat down next to my friends,
The teacher walked in,
She sat down and introduced herself;
I wasn't sure if I was going to get along with her.

The bell rang and the lesson was over,
I went to the Year 7 playground with my friends.
I stood there,
As older pupils went past they pushed and bumped into me.

We had three more lessons left,
The bell rang several more times, eventually school was over.
I was on the bus, it wasn't too bad.
I was thinking about my second day at school.

Sarah Knox (13)
Upton High School

My Dog, Patch!

I went to the house
Where he was,
Him and his brother,
Barking,
Playing,
Having fun.
I had to choose which one I wanted,
So I chose him,
The brown,
Playful,
Active one.

We named him Patch
And played all night.
He was cute, tiny and all mine.
As he got older, he grew bigger and stronger,
He went from tiny to large to in charge.

He knew what he wanted
And how he was going to get it,
But it didn't get him out of trouble.
Now he's gone and I miss him,
I'll never forget
My dog, Patch!

Roxanne Forster (13)
Upton High School

First Night Nerves

First night nerves
Two hours to go but it's started already
Over enthusiastic volunteers turn our faces orange
And then shout 'next' before we even stand up

Run to the changing room
Hiding clown-like faces until we reach the mirror
Manically grabbing tissues
A desperate attempt to make ourselves look 'normal'

Jump into costume
Vocal warm-up, physical warm-up
Trying to keep fidgety youths still and quiet
Finally, we're ready

Curtains, lights, band
Hearts racing, we're on
Moving across the stage
Like puppets on a string

Practised, precise, polished
Then, suddenly, it's over
Applause, bows, curtains
First night nerves turn into second night hysteria.

Kate Houlihan (16)
Upton High School

Shizilla, The Clown

Shizilla did hang on the rusty charity shop hook,
Waiting for bargain shoppers to pluck her from her loneliness,
Some drama students, acting the fools, spot Shizilla dangling
from the peg,
Shizilla is finally appreciated.

Shizilla has a new family, a strange arrangement of teenagers
of different heights and colours,
But not a colourful as Shizilla, with her soft painted clown face
and her stripy red and blue pyjamas.

She sleeps in a baby carrier nearly as soft as her,
Still her many parents look after the lifeless thing,
The performers have to play to act out, they must concentrate on
their cue lines, but what about Shizilla?

Shizilla is now alone!

It's the performers' last day. Music is played,
The actors all dance, it's a party!
A performer picks up the clown imitation doll,
They all cheer and reach for Shizilla.

Hungry hands grasp at her pyjamas, hundreds of eyes are fixed
on her red nose,
Shizilla is appreciated once more,
More cheers are screamed, more hands are reaching,
more eyes are looking

*Screaming, reaching, look*ing,
Shizilla! Shizilla! Shizilla!
Rip!

Shizilla's head is ripped off,
Fluffy stuffing is all over the floor,
Shizilla is dead! Appreciated no more!

Jonathan Young (16)
Upton High School

The Babysitter's Race

As I knock on the door
I judge my chances,
I'll give my best but there's tough competition,
Two small hands smack against the glass,
The race has begun.

First is the endurance test,
The plastic trucks and multicoloured toys are surrounding me,
Joined by the changing theme tunes screaming from the TV,
The finish seems a long way off.

I can feel my strength begin to fade,
There is one last hurdle before me,
I struggle over the baby-gate,
My competitor challenging me in my arms,
I prepare myself for the last lap.

The competition is not giving up easily,
I feel a last burst of strength,
The curtains are drawn and the light goes out,
I am victorious.

Stephanie Done (16)
Upton High School

Dark Nights

At night the streets go quiet,
At night the Earth is still,
At night the world is fast asleep,
Dreaming of frightening things.

It's terribly frightful at night!

At night the sun has set,
At night the moon shines bright,
At night the ghosts and ghouls come out,
With Dracula, demon and devil.

It's terribly frightful at night!

At night the fox chooses its prey,
At night the owls go hunting,
At night you hear such dreadful sounds,
That come time and time again.

It's terribly frightful at night!

But as the sun begins to rise
And the Earth begins to wake,
The world is a colourful, joyous place,
When the Earth is wide awake.

Charlotte Robinson (12)
Upton High School

Do This, Do That!

Do this, do that,
Don't act the prat.

Do well at school,
Don't be a fool.

Sit down, turn round,
Don't make a sound.

That's all they seem to say,
Can't they shut up just for one single day!

Go to your room,
Watch a cartoon.

You're impolite,
Get out of sight!

You're a disgrace,
You think you're ace!

That's all they seem to say,
Can't they shut up just for one single day!

Michael Bladen (14)
Upton High School

Life

I'm so tired of being alone
So tired of being here
So tired of being suppressed by all my immense fears

Walking round I see so many faces with no names
None of them know me or want to share my pain
There's nothing left to gain

Put under the pressure of walking in their shoes
I'm tired of being what they want me to be
What is it they expect of me?

As the days go on I walk on eggshells
People stare as I live my life in vain
So many players you'd think I was a ball game

Shame on you if you fool me once
Shame on me if you fool me twice
Shame on me, my life's a game, let's roll the dice

So concerned in what you think to just say what I feel inside
All I want is to feel that I'm not stepped on
Is there anybody out there or am I the only one?

There are so many things you say that make me feel you cross the line
I get stronger as the years go by
I can't get worse if I try

Anything you can do I can do better
All the pain gathered inside, a bomb waiting to explode
Should I let it all out or should I slowly implode?

No longer letting fear consume me
The bomb will go off, just say the word and I'll go
Trust me I'm stronger than you know.

Rachel Charnock (13)
Upton High School